# SALES QUESTIONS THAT CLOSE THE SALE

# SALES QUESTIONS THAT CLOSE THE SALE

## HOW TO UNCOVER YOUR CUSTOMERS' REAL NEEDS

**CHARLES D. BRENNAN, Jr.**

## amacom

**American Management Association**

New York • Atlanta • Boston • Chicago • Kansas City • San Francisco • Washington, D.C.
Brussels • Mexico City • Tokyo • Toronto

This publication is designed to provide accurate and authoritative information in regard to the subject matter covered. It is sold with the
understanding that the publisher is not engaged in rendering legal,
accounting, or other professional service. If legal advice or other ex-
pert assistance is required, the services of a competent professional
person should be sought.

Library of Congress Cataloging-in-Publication Data

Brennan, Charles D.
    Sales questions that close the sale : how to uncover your
customers' real needs / Charles D. Brennan, Jr.
        p.   cm.
    Includes index.
    ISBN 0-8144-7815-8
    1. Selling.   I. Title.
HF5438.25.B728   1994
    658.85—dc20                                    94-1054
                                                      CIP

Printing number

10  9  8  7  6  5  4  3

To Charles D. Brennan Sr., a friend, father, and mentor. A role model and leader who has helped shape my life and career. Thanks for all of the love and confidence and for providing me with a unique opportunity in life. Love, Dan

# Contents

# *Preface*

My father is a salesman. He spent the first decades of his professional life working for others and then opened his own very successful rep company. In fact he still travels throughout three states calling on refineries, chemical plants, and mechanical contractors for the half dozen manufacturers he represents.

I am a salesman too. I suspect this may sound corny, but I remember making my first sale. I was in the sixth or seventh grade, and I had received an electric football game as a gift. It was very popular at the time. Each game came with several NFL teams, but that wasn't enough for me. I was determined to field teams representing the league's entire roster.

Getting the other teams turned out to be surprisingly simple, a matter of horse-trading with friends, giving away little of value in exchange for valuable teams like the Chicago Bears, the Baltimore Colts (it *was* quite a few years ago), and the Los Angeles Rams. I don't recall exactly what I offered my playmates in return, but what I do remember vividly is the look on my father's face when he told my mother about my skills: "That boy can sell anything to anyone."

I'll bet I don't have to explain my emotions at that moment to anyone who is a salesperson. Chances are, especially since you're reading this book, that you've probably experienced the same sensations. Not only had I closed the deal, but I'd been recognized for it too. I had this overwhelming feeling of pride, accomplishment, and power. I'm not certain if that's when I decided to pursue a career in sales, though I suspect it played a role in my choice. A very significant role.

The truth is I think I would have become a salesperson

even if I hadn't managed to snare every National Football League team of the time. I think sales is in my blood. Again, at the risk of sounding corny, I believe great salespeople are born. I'm convinced they close their deals instinctively, similar to the way Ted Williams hit a belt-high fastball or O. J. Simpson weaved his way through onrushing tacklers, the way Billie Jean King smashed a crosscourt overhead. It's not something that can be taught.

## Improving Your Abilities to the Maximum

Coming from me, certainly, that may surprise you. After all, I make my living as head of the Sales Development Institute, a company that specializes in *training* salespeople. Not only that, but you've just plunked down a nice piece of change for a book that is supposed to show you how to improve your sales skills.

Well, read on. While I believe you cannot *learn* how to sell, I also believe that you can be *taught* to better use the tools of salesmanship you possess to better direct your natural skills toward closing the sale. Ted Williams and O. J. didn't just make it into the big leagues in a vacuum. Their skills were refined and improved by a series of coaches, beginning with Little League.

This book is about making you a better salesperson, about making you the Ted Williams, the O. J., the Billie Jean of your company. It's based on extensive research—my own and from other sources—as well as what I've learned from coming into contact with the literally thousands of people who have taken the Sales Development Institute courses over the last decade plus the thousands of sales calls I've made.

What these experiences have taught me is that selling is a constantly evolving vocation. Moreover, not only is selling changing, but the marketplace we serve is changing as well. Dramatically.

## Avoiding Jurassic Sales Park

And if we as salespeople don't change with it, we're going to be relegated to our version of a "Jurassic Sales Park." I offer you an option, a different approach to selling, that I am convinced will carry us into the twenty-first century and beyond.

For many of you, it will be a dramatically different approach to our craft. For some it will require only minor modifications in your current selling patterns. But if experience is any indication, everyone who adopts the principles outlined here will begin to see improvements in their ability to understand people and build relationships that close sales.

At the very heart of the system is my belief that the ability to build a relationship between vendor and customer, to make the selling experience a partnership, and to involve your client is the difference between success and failure. No, there's nothing dramatically new or complicated here. I didn't wake up one morning and yell, "Eureka!" Most of the concepts I'm going to introduce in this book are just good common sense. But when you get right down to it, isn't that exactly what good business practices are?

Before I get too modest, there are several features of the Sales Development Institute's approach that I believe to be particularly innovative. The first is the way a sales call is paced, a way that keeps you from going to Point C from Point A, without going through Point B. Something else unique about our approach is the way we go about building relationships and understanding sales prospects—by the simple expedient of asking the right questions. These are special questions, properly framed and targeted, to guide clients in a specific direction to recognize the need for change. They are intended to provide you with the kinds of answers you need. Ideally, these answers will help you to first identify your prospects' pain and then to come up with a viable solution for easing that pain. Finally, these answers will move the sales process along.*

## Believing in Yourself and What You Do

The system SDI uses is simple and easy to adapt to any industry. Yet our surveys indicate that 80 percent of all salespeople

*For more information on public and private seminars, call the Sales Development Institute, 1-800-220-7341.

don't ask the right questions partly, I suspect, because they haven't been taught how. As part of a complete consultative approach to selling, the right questions should stand out and make you stand out from the field too.

This consultative approach requires that you possess a certain mind-set, a belief in your own skills, as well as a commitment to your profession, your product, and your customer. It also requires that you understand that good sales calls have a certain rhythm. It's a rhythm that good salespeople can control. They, not the client, pace the sales call. In the next few chapters, I'm going to talk about the building blocks of relationship selling and how to make your customer your *partner* and not your *adversary*.

You will see just how easy this approach is. Thousands of participants like you go through our training program every year, and the results are occasionally staggering. (They will, of course, be described in detail in the pages to come.) All you have to do is approach this philosophy with an open mind. And read on.

# *Acknowledgments*

To my mother, for her confidence, love, support, and understanding as I developed as a person and professional.

To my wife, Annette, and children, Amanda and Daniel, for their continuous love, encouragement, support, and perseverance now and during the development of my abilities, my business, and this book.

To my clients who supported me at the beginning: Donald DeLess, Karen Cornelius, Phil Fannan, and Linda Taylor for their dedication and belief in my programs and concepts.

To those who have contributed their time and experience for the completion of this book: Michael McNeill, Michael Ludwig, Mark Besca, Daren Connelly, James Still.

To Andrea Pedolsky, for reading the article that made this book a reality and for her patience and assistance in the development of my book.

To coauthor, Curt Schleier, for doing a great job of listening to my ideas and introducing new ones in the writing and finalizing of my book.

To my colleague, Dolores, for staying with me all these years.

# SALES QUESTIONS THAT CLOSE THE SALE

# Chapter 1

## Selling With Commitment

If I use a single word more frequently than any other when I talk about my program, that word is change.

For all salespeople, of course, the ultimate goal is to get the buyers they call on to *change* their habits, to drop an existing supplier and deal with them instead. For this program to work, salespeople must first recognize the many *changes* in the business environment around them. And, as a result, they have to *change* not only the way they sell but often their entire mind-set about their job.

Certainly, changes in the business environment—in the way many, if not most, companies conduct business—are obvious. Or at least they ought to be obvious. After all, you can't pick up the business section of a newspaper or a business magazine without reading at least one article about the new global economy, temporary layoffs and permanent cutbacks, plant closings, lower budgets for marketing or research, and over-leveraged buyouts.

### Downsizing and Corporate Change

Even the large corporations everyone once thought immune to the vagaries of the world economy—the IBMs, the General Electrics, the P&Gs—have been forced into cutbacks and now conduct their affairs far differently from the way they did in the "go-go" years of the 1980s.

Yes, downsizing is a way of life, and it means that everyone, buyer and seller, has to do more with less—less time, less

1

energy to handle the myriad extra responsibilities heaped on a smaller staff, and fewer resources. But the changes go well beyond downsizing. The marketplace has become far more competitive, and that, too, has changed the old rules.

Consider that frequently in today's marketplace there is no discernable difference in the products and services offered by competing companies, and often there's no difference in price, either. Whether you sell chemicals, filters, computers, insurance, or real estate, Product A generally is Product A whether it's made by your company or the competition. And if you slash the price on Product A, chances are your competitor will match your cut before the ink is dry on the official announcement.

I know that when I make these statements, I am in many cases generalizing too much and oversimplifying. However, even if I exaggerate a bit, my point remains valid. And that point is, when everything else (for example, the products themselves and the price) is equal, or close to equal, the customer is going *to buy the salesperson.*

How can you take advantage of this new sales environment? How can you manipulate the changed circumstances to your benefit? The first thing you have to do is to determine what you have the power to control. Can you change the competitive factors in the marketplace that have an impact on your customers? No. Can you change what the competition is doing? Of course not. Can you change your company's management? No. No. No.

The only thing you can really change is you. In the Bible Jesus says, "Physician, heal thyself." It's a little presumptuous of me, but Charlie Brennan is saying, "Salesperson, change thyself."

I've come to recognize that, for salespeople, change is not always easy. A friend of mine is a consultant in the hot field of sales force automation. If you use a computer to augment your sales efforts, it's probably due to the efforts of my buddy, or someone very much like him, who goes into a corporation, examines its sales culture, and suggests hardware and software solutions to sales and marketing problems.

According to him, the toughest part of the process isn't

getting the funding. It isn't picking the proper laptop. And it isn't deciding whether or not to go with customized or off-the-shelf software. The biggest hurdle facing companies that want to automate their sales force is getting the training right and convincing salespeople to give computers a try.

As we all know, salespeople tend to be very independent. They can be set in their ways. It's not unusual for a salesperson to say, "Look, I've been doing okay without computers" and "I don't need anything to complicate my life."

At first, I was skeptical about what he told me. Sure, whenever I gave my seminars, there were always a few participants who held back and resisted my best efforts to introduce them to a new approach. But until my consultant friend made his comments, I wasn't aware of how widespread that resistance actually was. Then I started to notice it far more often.

For example, about a week after this conversation (which took place in the late 1980s), I conducted a training program for a group of salespeople who throughout most of their careers with their company sold a unique, almost monopolistic, product. Now the company faced competition, and the sales and marketing executives asked me to come in to reorient the sales staff.

It was a painful experience. The salespeople were all salaried employees. Their average age was somewhere in the early to mid-fifties. They had spent all their careers being reactive, calling on existing accounts. New business came to them; they never went out to seek it. For many, this was the first time in their professional lives that they were being asked to take a proactive approach to sales. To put it mildly, they didn't like it.

They'd grown comfortable in their nine-to-five jobs, they were all putting in their time until they retired, and now they felt their comfortable lives were in jeopardy. They lost sleep, they fought the change, and they kept returning to their old ways.

After awhile, some caught on to the concept I was trying to introduce. But many didn't. I still work for that company, and frankly, the majority of the people who fought me the hardest in the classroom, the ones most dead set against change, are no longer with the company. I'm not suggesting

that they're gone because they refused to adopt my philosophy. But I am suggesting that they may have lost their jobs
because they resisted any change at all. They failed to adapt to
the realities of the new marketplace.

A lot of salespeople are being forced to go from reactive to
proactive selling, and attempting to ignore that fact will not
alter it. Deregulation of former monopolies and increased competition have changed the way smart salespeople operate and
have made dumb ones redundant.

## Having an Image Problem

What do I mean by change? Every time I give a seminar I conduct the following exercise with the participants: Imagine that
you're at a cocktail party. Your assignment is to walk up to
twenty strangers and ask them what adjectives come to mind
when they hear the word *salesperson*. I tell the class to write the
word down and within seconds, pens and pencils are flying.
The results? They're not surprising—words like: *sleazy, pushy,
obnoxious, loud, fast talkers.*

In part, it's an image that's perpetuated by the media.
Willy Loman, the sad sack, in Arthur Miller's brilliant play,
*Death of a Salesman*, the aluminum siding salesmen in the film
*Tin Men*, the real estate salesmen in the play, turned film, *Glen-
garry Glen Ross*, even Herb, the ad salesman in the television
show *WKRP in Cincinnati* all are people in our profession who
are portrayed in an extremely negative light. But the image of
salespeople goes beyond the myths created by the media. At
some time in our lives, many of us have met the old "slap on
the back, cigar smoking, sale at any cost" salesperson, the car-
icature the media delights in so much. When I ask the class if
they've ever met someone like that, everyone's head nods in
recognition. Perhaps it was at a retail store or showroom, or it
may have been a business-to-business salesperson who'd called
on them.

Then I ask the class how many of them had friends who
might just as easily have the same opinions of salespeople as
the guests at that fictional cocktail party. Typically, everyone

indicates that they know people who hold these negative opinions. I even have friends who use derogatory adjectives about salespeople, and they're lawyers.

Finally, I ask the participants to raise their hands if they, themselves, might have used the same, or similar, expressions when referring to a salesperson. I honestly cannot remember the last time that less than 90 percent of the participants didn't raise their hands, acknowledging that, yes, those adjectives have come to their minds, too, about some salespeople. That's when I pounce. If *you* have those thoughts about salespeople, *you* a salesperson yourself and *you* a person who knows the difficulties of cold calls and rejections, if *you* have those thoughts about salespeople, then what do you think is on your customers' minds when you approach them? What do you think *they're* thinking?

We all know that those negative adjectives aren't accurate. Yet we get called those names because, traditionally, salespeople have emphasized selling and closing. You ask, isn't that what we are supposed to do? Perhaps this was so in the past when competition was less fierce, and we all lived in our version of a *Field of Dreams:* "If you build it, they will come—and *buy* it." Clearly, times are different now. The field of dreams has now become a nightmare: "If you build it, someone else will build it cheaper or differently and find some other way to keep you from making the sale."

But let's forget about selling for a moment. Think about your closest friends. Write down the adjectives that best describe your relationship with them. If you're at all like the people who have attended my seminar, chances are that one word will keep cropping up time and time again. That word is *trust*. Other words that come up with great regularity are *honest, caring, supportive,* and *common interests*.

During my seminars, I wonder out loud how long it takes to build this kind of relationship, and obviously the most common answer I receive is *years*. It takes time to get to know someone, to learn their likes and dislikes, and how they're likely to respond in a variety of situations. Obviously, we salespeople are a lot better off when our clients and prospects feel sufficiently comfortable to describe us using the friendship adjectives rather than with the negative adjectives that describe traits normally attributed to salespeople. However, to get that kind of positive description, something clearly has to give.

## A Four-Part Commitment to Selling

The first thing that has to change is that negative image of salespeople. Today's business environment requires that you do what I call "sell with commitment." You may refer to it as a holistic approach to selling. Some people have called it a "New Age" approach. But no matter how you label it, it's just good business. What is this approach? It's actually a four-part commitment you must make:

  • *First, you have to make a commitment to your company.* They say a good salesperson can sell anything. That's not true. A good salesperson can only sell what he or she believes in and is enthusiastic about. Salespeople who try to sell without conviction generate the kinds of negative comments I've just discussed.

  • *Second, you have to make a commitment to your job.* You have to recognize that selling is a profession, and it exists in an evolving environment. What worked yesterday doesn't work today. Doctors, accountants, engineers, lawyers, and other professionals are frequently required to enroll in continuing education programs to keep their accreditation or licenses, and that has to somehow be mirrored in sales. Individually and as a group, we have to resolve to stay abreast of developments in sales, in general, and our industries, in particular. The simple fact is that past successes don't guarantee future performance. But persistence, constant striving for knowledge, and refining existing talents will.

I frequently tell a story I first heard a long time ago, a story that is almost certainly apocryphal. It's about the president of a large company and one of his salespeople. They meet at a company function, and the salesman's peers are surprised at how chummy the two are.

The salesman explains to his friends regarding the president, "We first got to know each other when we started with the company together as salesmen. It was on the same day, twenty-five years ago." His friends ask him, "How come he became president, and you're still in sales?" According to the salesman who stayed a salesman, "When I joined the company, I wanted to earn a paycheck. But my friend, he wanted to earn a career." I said it was an apocryphal story. When I first heard it, I didn't believe it either. But I eventually got the point.

- *Third, you have to make a commitment to your client.* You have to act in your customer's best interest, and that means having the strength to walk away from a deal when it's not in his or her best interest. You have to focus on your customer's long-term needs and not your own short-term gain.

- *Finally, and most important of all, you have to make a commitment to yourself.* You must recognize that you are in absolute control of your life. How you spend your time, how you educate yourself, and how you develop your activities to their utmost are up to you. Too often, salespeople shift blame. They assert, "I didn't get an order because the price was wrong," or "I didn't get the support I needed." Those excuses don't cut it.

If you call on a customer with a selling-with-commitment attitude that says, "I am in control; I can engage you in a better relationship than anyone else, and I can precipitate a change in your buying habits," then you are going to make that sale, or at least have a good shot at it. I know this sounds kind of pie-in-the-sky. But the plain fact is that in today's business environment, the most important ingredient in the sales mix is the salesperson. And if you don't believe in yourself, your customer won't either. I'll say this again and again: "The key is building a good working, professional relationship." The emphasis there is on a *professional*, rather than on an old-fashioned, "let me give you a cigar and buy a round of drinks" type of relationship.

## Buyers Agreeing That You're the Key

I conducted an informal study for the Sales Development Institute (SDI) in which I asked a group of buyers in a variety of industries to rate a number of factors that influence their purchasing decisions. The number one answer was that their relationship with the salesperson was the most important factor, followed by product quality, and past successes with the product. All things being equal, they were impressed by the salesperson, who was understanding and caring.

I believe the results of the study are interesting in that they reflect the realities of the new marketplace. Moreover, they appear to be universal in the marketplace. Whether you're selling jet planes or fountain pens and no matter what technical advances have been made in your industry, people still buy people, which includes buying relationships, trust, understanding, and caring.

Still, some people in my training course remained skeptical. They gave me a lot of grief when I mentioned the results of the survey. Or at least they gave me grief until I tried to personalize the survey. I told them a story about a patient, call him Joe, who goes to an orthopedist complaining about back pain. The doctor examines Joe briefly, for no more than five minutes, and then tells him that he will need surgery. Wisely, Joe decides to get a second opinion.

Doctor Two also examines Joe and asks about his medical history, his activities, and his life-style. All told, Dr. Two spends about an hour with Joe. Then he orders X-rays, a CAT scan, and magnetic resonance tests. He takes the results of all those tests to three other experts in the field to get their input. A week later he calls Joe back and gives him the news: He's going to need surgery.

I asked the participants to play the role of Joe: "Which of these physicians will you trust with your back? The doctor who quickly examined you or the one who took his time, got to know you, and brought in other professionals to seek their guidance too?" Almost invariably, all the "Joes" in my classes select Dr. Two.

My next question is: "Which one is the more competent doctor? The one who was able to determine the need for surgery quickly, without wasting a lot of time or money on expensive tests or the one who went through an expensive and time-consuming process only to reach the same conclusion?" Dr.

One might indeed be the superior doctor, but he or she didn't get the business. The moral of this tale is that you have to have the salesperson's equivalent of a good bedside manner. You have to listen and learn because the bottom line is that if you have two comparable products (and that is the reality of the new marketplace), you will probably buy from the salesperson who has the better bedside manner.

## Avoiding the Traditional Sales Approach

Unfortunately, building a better relationship has never been a priority in what I call the traditional sales approach. See Figure 1-1. In the traditional approach, salespeople spent only 10 percent of their time building rapport with their clients, 20 percent discovering the customer's needs, 30 percent making presentations, and 40 percent trying to close the deal. The main emphasis in this approach was on selling and closing, not listening

**Figure 1-1.** The traditional sales approach.

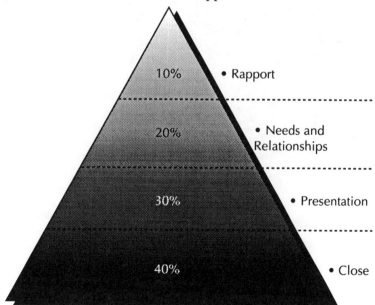

- 10% • Rapport
- 20% • Needs and Relationships
- 30% • Presentation
- 40% • Close

and learning and becoming a partner with your prospect. Those percentages might have been in the right proportion in a go-go business environment when the close is the desired result, and if this prospect doesn't buy, you move on quickly, because there's another one waiting with a purchase order ready.

Of course, it doesn't work that way anymore. Salespeople have to ignore the short-term and take a long-range view. In the consultative selling approach (see Figure 1-2) salespeople spend 40 percent of their time listening, communicating, and building rapport. They spend 30 percent of their time initiating a professional relationship, and understanding and developing the customer's needs. Then they spend only 20 percent of their time on a presentation and 10 percent on the close. The defining element of this approach is reaching the understanding that the buyer and seller are not adversaries. Rather their working together for solutions builds rapport, confidence, and ultimately orders.

**Figure 1-2.** The consultative selling approach.

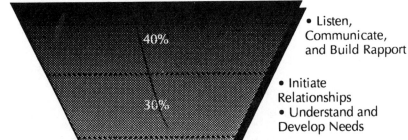

The way to communicate the consultative approach is the defining element of this book. For example, a study by the University of California at Los Angeles attempted to gauge the importance of three factors that influence communication: the words being said, vocal elements (the way you say something and your tone of voice), and nonverbal factors. On a percentage basis, which of these three factors do you think was rated highest? Next highest? And which do you think finished last?

Usually when I ask people these questions, anywhere between 20 and 70 percent answer what you've probably answered: Your words are the most important. However, according to the UCLA study, only 7 percent of people are influenced by words. Moreover, 38 percent are affected by your tone. But by far the single largest factor in communication, the one rated most important, is your nonverbal body language.

At first that surprised me too. But the more I thought about it, I realized how someone's passion and emotion can make it easier to transfer an idea. I don't know if you saw the film *Dead Poet's Society*, but Robin Williams jumping up on a desk to teach comes immediately to mind here.

Of course, salespeople can't jump on a desk to make their points. So typically they rely on other tools (the wrong ones) to get their message across. Consider the typical sales call. Your harried prospect ushers you into an office, and he or she starts the conversation off with something like:

- "I've only got ten minutes. Tell me what you've got."
- "I'm satisfied with my current supplier."
- "Your price is too high."
- "I've tried you in the past and had a bad experience."

That leaves even the best salesperson only one option—to quickly rebut this point. For example:

- "Here's what we have."
- "We're better than the other guy."
- "I can make you a deal."
- "It will never happen again."

But there are numerous problems with this rebuttal. First of all, you're using words. And if the UCLA study is correct (and I believe it is), words are the least effective way to get your point across.

Worse yet, because you've allowed your prospect to control the direction of the call, he's put you in the position of engaging in a one-way conversation instead of conducting a dialogue that will lead to increased levels of trust.

In the next few chapters, I'm going to discuss such factors as how to get the call off to a proper start, how to pace yourself, and how to avoid losing control of the call. Then, most important, I'm going to discuss the art of questioning, the different kinds of questions there are, the different responses they generate, and how to ask the right kinds of questions that lead to a true dialogue.

# Chapter 2

## *Pacing the Call*

As a rule, good salespeople do a decent job opening sales calls. After all, we tend to be gregarious by nature, enjoying the company of others and building relationships easily. If not, we would be monks, or bosses. But in the new marketplace, just building a relationship is no longer enough. How you build your relationship, how you differentiate yourself from other salespeople, how you pace your call, and how you control it are of paramount importance.

There are three factors at play here that have mandated changes in a good salesperson's approach and outlook. First, and most important, is the cutbacks that have affected virtually every industry in the country. The odds are probably very good that the person you are calling on is handling 50 percent more work than he or she did in the late 1980s because cutbacks have eliminated several peers and the support personnel that used to sit at nearby desks or in nearby offices. But those people's responsibilities haven't been eliminated. They've just been distributed amongst the survivors.

As a result, your prospect is pressed for time and less interested in the kind of idle chatter that used to pass for rapport-building conversation to open sales calls in the good old days.

The second factor is the financial pressures weighing upon companies. There was a time in the "go-go" years of the mid-1980s when entire industries thought they were extensions of the United States Mint. They spent money almost as though they'd been awarded a license to print it. If you couldn't make a full run sale, chances were you could at least get a prospect to try your product or service or to buy a short run to see how well it worked.

Of course, those days have gone the way of the dodo bird. Today money is tight. Upper management expects every dollar, every penny, to be well spent. This is putting increased pressure on every department, and, in turn, the people responsible for making purchases are putting increased pressure on suppliers. The watchwords now are *return on investment*.

Finally, the third factor is an almost natural resistance to change which I alluded to in the previous chapter. This is a variation of the "if it ain't broke, don't fix it" philosophy, even if fixing it will help make work go more smoothly. It's not a big secret that inertia is often present, even in the best of economic times, within the bureaucracy of large corporations. And let's be honest, inertia is present in small companies as well. In both cases, as the financial picture deteriorates, a don't-make-waves mind-set takes on tidal wave proportions. While this works to our benefit when it comes to existing accounts—buyers prefer the status quo and are unlikely to sign on new vendors—it works against us when we're trying to land new business.

## A Model for Pacing Your Sales Call

Attaining greater penetration into existing accounts is certainly a large part of what we as salespeople do. However, landing new business is really what the sales "game" is all about. Yet, what is often overlooked in this equation is that we also have pressures. We, too, may be survivors of layoffs, working larger territories and handling more accounts. Our supervisors are also watching what we do more closely than they used to, and the distance from the sales floor to the exit door is shrinking all the time. There is no such thing as a safe sinecure any longer. This means we have to use our time more judiciously. To do that, I have developed what I call the quarter-half-quarter model. See Figure 2-1.

The quarter-half-quarter model is a guide that enables individuals to properly pace themselves during the sales call. Showing when to apply the five phases of consultative selling,

**Figure 2-1.** The five phases of consultative selling.

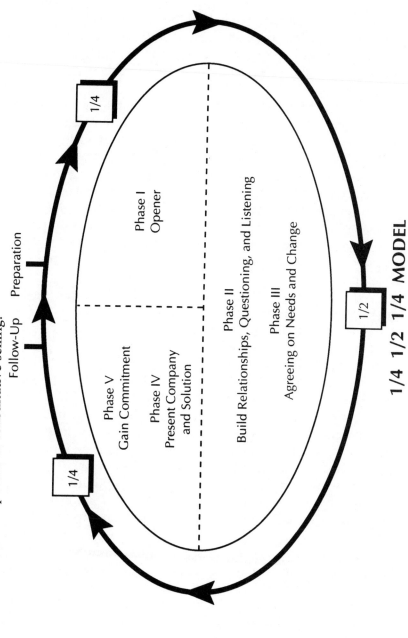

Follow-Up

Preparation

Phase I
Opener

Phase II
Build Relationships, Questioning, and Listening

Phase III
Agreeing on Needs and Change

Phase V
Gain Commitment

Phase IV
Present Company
and Solution

1/4

1/2

1/4

1/4 1/2 1/4 MODEL

the model provides the sequence and emphasis required for each phase during the selling process. Based on consultative selling, the model requires half of the time typically spent with a prospective client in phases II and III (building relationships, questioning, and agreeing on needs and change). The remaining time with the prospect is to be balanced between opening the call and closing it.

In this model, the first quarter of the actual sales call itself, the opener, is where you introduce yourself, create some kind of common ground, state the reason for your visit, gain the prospect's interest, and state your goal. The half, which will be discussed in greater detail in upcoming chapters, is where you learn, listen, ask questions (I'll be going into substantial detail about various kinds of questions), and build the relationship and client interest. And the final quarter is where you present solutions, summarize the benefits of your products or services, respond to any objections, and gain commitments to move closer to the sale.

What I think you'll find appealing about the quarter-half-quarter model is that it's fluid. Because it isn't absolute or fixed, it is easily adaptable to your business and your industry's sales cycle. It recognizes that getting a commitment from a prospect won't necessarily happen on your first sales call.

In fact, a study by the New York Sales and Marketing Club indicates that sales are typically closed on the fifth call. The sales cycle, of course, varies from industry to industry and from salesperson to salesperson. But whatever your personal sales cycle is, the percentage of time you spend on a particular aspect of a call will change, sometimes dramatically, depending upon how far along in the cycle you are (see Figure 2-2).

All three sections of the model occur on every call, but the emphasis shifts as your relationship with the prospect matures. For example, you will always be expected to prepare for a call and the opening will vary from only a few minutes up to, but not exceeding, one quarter of your time. However, as you get to know and establish a rapport with your client, you'll spend less time in the "Building Relationship" portion of the model, and more in the "Presenting Solution" and "Gaining Commitment" segment of the sales cycle.

**Figure 2-2.** Applying the 1/4-1/2-1/4 model during the sales cycle.

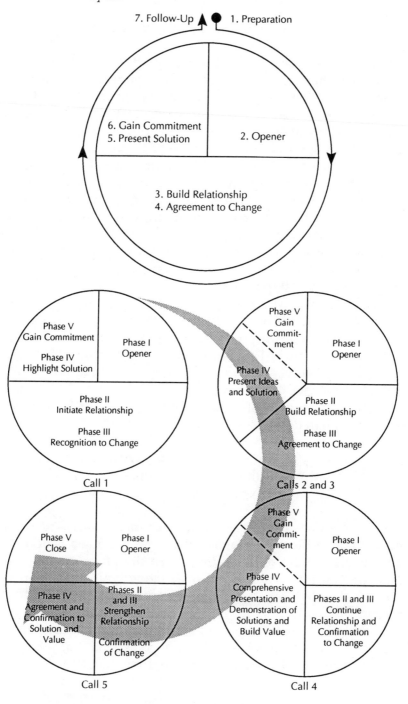

## The Salesperson as Consultant

Before going into detail about the first quarter of your sales call, the opener, there are a couple of points that need to be emphasized. One of the most important details, one that needs to constantly be at the front of your mind every time you visit a prospect or customer, is that the driving principle behind every sales call is that you want to be viewed as a partner.

At the heart of the consultative approach, you function as a consultant, not as a salesperson. Like a good consultant, you are there to create a win-win situation for everyone, not just to close a deal. Also like a good consultant, you're there to listen to your client's problems, not to provide snap answers. You want to study and learn the prospects' buying processes, you want to diagnose his or her needs, and you want to build a long-term relationship with trust.

So anything that pushes you into the sales mode too soon, anything that forces you to regress into the traditional sales mode defeats your purpose and makes you appear to be just another salesperson. This brings me to my second point: You have to maintain control of the meeting, so you're not forced into a traditional sales mode.

And being pushed into a traditional sales mode is easy. We discussed them in the last chapter:

- "I've only got ten minutes. Tell me what you've got."
- "I'm satisfied with my current supplier."
- "I've had a bad experience."

There are a dozen or more similar statements a prospect can make to open the conversation which can become a Pandora's box for you. The problem is that when the prospect starts off pushing you into a traditional sales mode, you, the salesperson, are diverted from a building-a-relationship mode. Rather, you are almost literally forced into the "Presenting Solutions" quarter, bypassing the most important part of the quarter-half-quarter model which is the half where you spend time building and nurturing a relationship based on understanding.

Moreover, in the traditional sales mode you are answering

in words, and, as we discussed in the last chapter, that is the least effective way to communicate your point. In fact, in this mode, you're operating at a 93 percent failure rate. Finally, you are no longer able to steer the conversation in a way that presents you as being different from other salespeople. Instead, you are forced into giving traditional kinds of answers that are likely to be very identical to the responses your prospect received from your competitors.

## The Five-Step First Quarter Model

In order to be in control of the meeting, I suggest a five-step opening that may *seem* similar to what you do now, but is actually very different in its approach. This first quarter is intended to focus the call and make the proper impression on your client, so it is critical that each of these steps be followed. As you'll see, there's a kind of natural progression to them and eliminating one, throws off the synergy of the entire model. It begins with:

1. *The introduction*. Don't expect any magic here. You introduce yourself, the company you represent, and offer a brief, thirty second explanation of what you do. Caution: Don't go into too much detail here. Too much detail might open the door for your prospect to ask a question or make a statement that will force you into the final quarter and a traditional, rather than a consultative, sales call. For example, suppose in describing your company, you say something as innocent and simple as, "We've been in the business for over sixty years and have hundreds of satisfied customers." The prospect might say, "Well, I just spoke to Joe Blow, and quite frankly, he told me that he wasn't happy with your product at all."

At that point, you have no choice but to somehow try to defend the efficacy of your product which automatically takes you out of the first quarter and out of the consultative selling approach. So *keep it simple*. The less said, the better!

2. *Statement of common ground*. Every modern sales course and every modern sales manager offers pretty much the same

advice for starting a sales call. I call it the "I'm really sincere and I care about you" formula. It's basic psych 101.

The idea is that you want to build rapport with the client and show him or her that you are not mercenary, but a true friend. "Whoa!" you may say at this point. "Is that what *you* want us to do?" Yes, it is. Sort of.

Actually, you're not really there to be the prospect's personal friend. I quarrel with the usual approach to building a relationship. At best, you're there to become, in part, a *business* friend. The conversation during your first sales call should be kept on a *business* level, but it usually isn't. Typically, a salesperson comes in and looks around the prospect's office for some way to make a connection—a photo, an award, a trophy—any artificial way to start a conversation.

Let's just say that you are the fifth of five new bidders on a project who've all made a face-to-face sales call in one day. Each of you has walked into the prospect's office to discover a large and very impressive stuffed swordfish mounted proudly behind the client's desk. Beneath the fish is a photograph of the prospect looking very proud, a boat captain, also looking proud, and that fish, the object of their affection, hanging hook in mouth, looking slightly less than proud. I'd be willing to bet that you will probably be the fifth person to start the conversation with some comment about the fish:

> "Did you catch that?"
> "Where did you catch that monster?"
> "You know, I'm a fisherman, too."

As a result, in your attempt to build a relationship, you are unintentionally breeding insincerity. And the same is true when you comment on the picture of his (or her) kids or his (or her) bowling trophy.

By no means am I suggesting that you not be observant. After all, the prospect didn't put that fish up there for you to ignore. But if you open the conversation the way everyone else does, you will wind up being viewed as just another salesperson, the same as the other four who already called on the prospect. And since you're the last one in, the same opening gambit will probably put you at a disadvantage.

I tell people that, yes, you have to establish a common ground, but that common ground has to be on a business level, not on a personal level. On an initial meeting especially, you should be discussing business issues, such as the market, industry trends, and the like rather than personal issues. That means you have to do your homework.

What do I mean by homework? I mean research into the prospect's company and particular industry. For example, if you sell in a vertical industry, such as airplane engines or chemicals, you probably keep up with the trade press on this industry, so you probably know what's going on in the industry overall and with the prospect's company in particular.

I say *probably* because ever since about 1990, I've asked participants in SDI courses how many of them read their industry's trade press, and the number of hands going up has consistently gone down. I am invariably surprised by how few people bother with their own industry's news. When I ask why, the responses I receive are almost always the same: "I just don't have time."

I understand this, to a certain degree. I know there are numerous times when I'm on the road for a week or more and come back to find my desk swamped under a deluge of mail, messages, and trade and consumer publications that overwhelms me. However, I slog through it all because I recognize that the race isn't necessarily won by the swiftest. In sales, it's usually won by the best prepared.

In fact, I suggest going beyond just the trade press. Certainly how far you go depends on the prospect's potential. But given the cost of a sales call today, even the smallest prospect ought to be worth a trip to the library. If it's a local company and it's big enough, the library may have copies of recent annual and quarterly reports that you can look at to see if there are any trends. That is the least you should do to prepare for a sales call.

In all likelihood, the company has been covered in the local newspaper. Its president or some other top officer may recently have made an important speech that has made an impact on the industry. There also may have been recent personnel changes that you should be aware of.

Even the smallest library probably has a computer hooked up to a regional database that lets you put in a company's name and pull up stories about the company that have appeared in major magazines and newspapers. You can do the same for the company's product and industry.

While most library computers only index major newspapers and national magazines, like *The New York Times*, *Time*, and *Newsweek*, for example, there are several private database systems that allow you to also call up articles that have appeared in a variety of local and regional magazines as well as a variety of business, trade, and technical publications.

If you can get your company to sign up with any one of several on-line database systems, you'll be able to actually print out these articles from your own office. These systems are expensive, but landing one new client can potentially pay for several year's worth of hookups. No matter how you secure the information, though, the basic principle is that you have to build up your own database on the client, partly because information is power, but mostly because it will set you apart from the herd.

Usually I'll bring a printout or photocopy of an article with me when I make a sales call and actually show it to the client. I may even mention it as we walk from the reception area to the client's office. If he or she hasn't seen it, I'll leave it with him or her (or have a photocopy made of it). If he or she has seen it, we can discuss it, and the prospect will know that I came to this sales call prepared.

For example, I recently called on an accounting firm, and I brought out an article that said large accounting firms were having a problem attracting entrepreneurial companies as clients. "That's true," the prospect said to me. "And that's one of our biggest challenges—getting in to see the chief executive or chief financial officer and establishing a relationship with them." Clearly the article achieved what I wanted it to:

- It sparked a conversation.
- It kept the prospect from saying something that would

push me into the "Presenting Solutions" phase of the call.

- It separated me from the competition.
- It showed I did my homework.
- It kept me in control.

The few minutes that I'd spent in the library paid substantial dividends. And I can give you literally dozens of examples of how an article I brought on a call opened up a conversational path that eventually led to a sale. I showed a real estate company executive an article in which a court held an agent liable for misrepresentation even though he presumed the comments he made to his client were true. It turned out that building real estate agent/client trust because of that case was one of this executive's "hot button" issues. At a chemical company, an article about how environmental issues were having an impact on its operations and products was a major issue that led first to a two-way conversation and ultimately to a sale.

Ideally, whatever article you duplicate and bring with you should not only somehow include your prospect's business but your product or service as well. For example, if you sell computer systems, you should try to find an article about automation or productivity. If you sell health care services, the article should be about the growing concern in the marketplace about the quality of care or rising costs. Obviously, the computer salesperson shouldn't bring an article about health care and vice versa.

It's an added bonus if the article presents information that's new to the prospect, but that's not critical. What is important is that you communicate that you walked the extra mile and the competition didn't. What you want your prospect to say is, "Gee, this is a refreshing approach. It's not just small talk."

3. *Stating the purpose of the call.* Once your homework, a newspaper or magazine article or whatever it is, establishes a conversation, the segue into starting the agenda for the call is usually almost effortless. When the prospect says, "Yes, that's one of the issues we're facing," how easy it is to say (as I sug-

gest): "Well, Mr. Johnson, that's why I'm here. I want to get a clear understanding of what your challenges are and how these issues have an impact on your company as well as to introduce you to some of the innovative things we're doing in the marketplace that might be helpful." What this does is set an agenda that, at this stage, is difficult to deviate from. It closely mirrors the consultative selling model. And finally it allows you to maintain control over the conversation.

Consider the example of the real estate agent I used earlier. When he said to me that the issue of trust between prospects and his salespeople was important to him, imagine how easy it was to segue into the training programs offered by the Sales Development Institute.

4. *Gaining client interest.* Once you've navigated this far, gaining client interest is actually a lot easier than you might suspect. One study suggests that a prospect can be influenced if you just use the word "because" and give a reason, even if the reason is nonsensical.

Obviously, I'm not suggesting that you say, "I believe we really ought to pursue this further because you have lovely green eyes." But if you say, ". . . because we've been able to help a lot of companies reduce their production costs or marketing costs," you probably have captured your prospect's heart and mind.

A "gain interest" statement is one that tells the prospect that you have done this sale successfully before and that it is well worth his or her time to spend a few minutes listening to what you have to say. The best "gain interest" statements are those that target one of the prospect's "hot button" issues.

5. *Introducing your objectives and expectations.* This last step in the opening phase of a sales call is of critical importance, yet it is often overlooked. It is extremely significant because, short of getting a signed contract, it is the only way to accurately gauge how well the meeting went.

Your objective is always to set up the next meeting, the next step in the cycle, and *it must always be measurable and specific.* Stating vague or noncommittal objectives such as, "build a better relationship," "generate interest," or "get back to you with more information" are common traps salespeople fall into. These objectives aren't measurable, and they don't require any action or genuine expressions of interest on the part of the prospect.

A measurable objective, on the other hand, can be something as simple as, "If things go well today, what I'd like to do is set up a demonstration for you next week." Or it can be something far more complicated, like inviting the prospect to a site inspection of your plant.

However, I know how disheartening it can be for a salesperson to go through an entire call believing everything is moving forward like gangbusters, only to be unable to secure a follow-up appointment. It is similarly frustrating for a sales manager to ask a salesperson how a call went and to hear, "Good" or "We're developing a good relationship." What does that mean? Will this relationship lead to an order, or are the salesperson and prospect merely going to become good friends? Clearly, an agreement to move on to the next step in the cycle is a measurable and positive step.

Yet, anyone who has known the frustration of trying to set up a second, third, and fourth appointment with a prospect is likely to say it is easier said, than done. Nevertheless, once you've gained a toehold, established a viable common ground with the prospect, and set yourself apart from the competition, the rest is easy. Because, chances are, your prospect will want to help you succeed. By stating this measurable objective early in your meeting and getting the prospect to agree to it during the first quarter, you have a course to steer, a rudder for you "sale-ing" ship, that keeps you "selling" in the right direction. To keep this nautical metaphor going, the objective also serves as an anchor, something solid to come back to at the end of the call: "As I said earlier, Mr. Prospect, I'd like to come back next week to give you a complete demonstration."

If the prospect doesn't agree with your agenda, it's still early enough in the process to find out why the prospect doesn't share your enthusiasm. It's perfectly all right to ask prospects what they had in mind when they made the appointment with you and what their intentions were.

In the next few chapters, I'll be talking about other facets of the sales call and how to pace it. We'll be discussing how to gauge the significance of your prospects' responses and, more important, how to ask the right kinds of questions—questions that help you strengthen your bond with the prospect, provide you with the information you need to clinch the sale, and differentiate you from the competition.

# Chapter 3

## *Some More First Quarter Tips*

I'm sure there are coaches who'll tell you that the first few innings, the first quarter, or the first set of a game are the most important because they set a tone for the entire competition. I believe this is true when it comes to sales calls also—to a point.

I'm sure any of you who are sports fans have seen an individual or a team dominate a game or a match until the last few minutes, only to collapse and lose. Similarly, the facets (each "period") of the quarter-half-quarter model are all important, and if you fail to follow any part of it, the whole may collapse.

But if there is one facet of the model that is more important than the others, it is the first quarter. Simply, if you don't make your way through this quarter successfully, you may not make it to the half. Unfortunately, the prospect can call the game at any time, rain or shine.

Constructing a good sales call is like constructing a sturdy building. There is a certain logic to it. You don't put up a roof without a foundation. The five-point opener presented in the previous chapter is a good example of what I call the model's building block logic: the way you can go from introduction to common ground to stating your purpose without forcing the issue. It seems as natural as casual conversation, and if it does not yet seem that way, I guarantee it will once you try it a few times and see how well it works.

## Practice Makes Perfect—A Testimonial

Typically, at this point in the seminar, I usually find a small pocket of resistance. I'll let Mike McNeill, sales manager of Forte Systems, Inc., Philadelphia, tell you about it.

Mike took my course at a previous job, and when he joined Forte, a systems integrator that sells to Fortune 500 accounts, he put his new sales force through the program. He told me after he put a dozen sales reps through the course, "The thing that they were most resistant to was that this methodology forces you to do certain things at certain times during a sales cycle, and that's sometimes uncomfortable for a few account executives to do."

He added, "A lot of account executives like to wing it and are uncomfortable being prepared. This is the only profession where people go out and actually practice in front of their customers. They like to get into a sales call, let it flow, and end up wherever it takes them.

I know. Before I took the course, there were plenty of times when I allowed my own overzealousness to disrupt sales calls. Now I pace my calls properly. What I especially like about the quarter-half-quarter methodology is that it always allows me to know where I am and to maintain control. Whether you use it as is or incorporate some of your own sales techniques, I don't think any of it is malarkey."

McNeill actually has his people practice the calls, including the questions they expect to ask, before they go out to meet their prospects. "It's part of the planning aspect," he explains. And it seems to be working. Forte is a privately held company, so he won't tell me actual figures. But he says his sales have been doubling every year, and the company was recently called one of the fastest-growing in Philadelphia. So I take his testimonial as a compliment.

Consider that this five-point program probably resembles much of what you are already doing. You don't have to modify your behavior a great deal in order to take advantage of the model I've created. It really is *almost* just as easy to create a bond by saying, "I just saw this interesting article . . ." as it is to say "What a big fish. . . ." I said almost. It requires a little extra work, but, again, that work will set you apart.

## First Quarter Simulations

As you can see, there is a natural flow to this sales process. It isn't artificial. I do a lot of role-playing in my seminars, and I can see how quickly participants master pacing their sales calls. This practice is not difficult to master, and after just one or two exercises, virtually everyone begins to feel comfortable. Here are some sample simulated openers for a first call:

### EXAMPLE 1

*Introduction:* Good morning, Mr. Prospect, my name is ———, of XYZ Company.

*Client response:* (cordial welcoming)

*Common ground:* In preparing for our meeting today, I did a little research on your industry and noticed a series of articles indicating a trend to consolidate. What has been your experience?

*Client response:* (information concerning consolidation)

*Agenda:* (state name of prospect), that's exactly why I'm here— to learn more about what you're experiencing and understand what initiated your proposal request along with some of the challenges you are currently facing. In addition, I would like to share with you information about our company.

*Gain interest:* Because of our involvement with businesses like yours, we have been able to help companies increase productivity and lower costs. This was my plan for our meeting today. Could you share yours?

*Client response:* (sounds fine)

*Objective:* If all goes well in our meeting today, and we feel that we have enough information about your business, I would like to speak with some of our specialists and schedule a meeting with them and any other individuals from your company involved in the decision-making process in the next week or so to review your situation.

———, is there anything else you would like to cover during our meeting?

## EXAMPLE 2

*Introduction:* Good morning, Mr. Prospect, my name is ———— of the ABC Phone Company.

*Client response:* (cordial welcoming)

*Common ground:* In preparing for our meeting today, I did a little research on the real estate industry in the area. I understand that the drop in interest rates has pumped new life into the market. What are you seeing in your coverage area?

*Client response:* (information concerning real estate activity)

*Agenda:* That's exactly why I'm here—to learn more about the challenges you are currently facing with regard to your phone system. I would like to share with you information about some of our products and services.

*Gain interest:* Because of our involvement with service industries, we have been able to provide communication systems to help companies operate more efficiently. This was my plan for our meeting today. Could you share yours?

*Objective:* If all goes well in our meeting today, and we feel that we have enough information about what you want to accomplish, I would like to schedule a meeting with you and anyone else involved in a week or two to present a communication systems proposal.

————, is there anything else you would like to review during our meeting?

## EXAMPLE 3

*Introduction:* Good morning, Mr. Client. My name is Joe West, representing Fortran Computer Systems Inc., a distributor of computer software and hardware products and services. Thanks for taking the time to meet with me today. I really appreciate the chance to learn more about you and your company.

*Client response:* (cordial welcoming)

*Common ground:* In preparing for our meeting today, I was reading a recent article in *Computer Age* magazine discussing the growing concern of end user demands. Have you seen this article, and does this affect you in your position?

*Client response:* I haven't seen the article, but this is certainly an issue that is starting to come to the forefront for us. With the increased amount of users and the advancement of products available, we are trying to keep up with technology, where necessary, and our end user demands, when valid.

*Sales rep:* You mentioned that it is starting to come to the forefront. What were some of the elements that prompted greater attention in this area?

*Client response:* Corporately, we are trying to streamline our operations and develop the capabilities as well as capacities of our personnel. To do this, we realize we need to automate certain areas as well as acquire software systems to allow us to function more effectively in our operations.

*Sales rep:* You mentioned you are trying to keep up with technology where necessary and meet the requests of end user demands when valid. It sounds as if you recognize the importance of upgrading and expanding your systems, but you need to manage the expectations of your end users. How is that balancing process going?

*Client response:* I think you are pretty accurate in your assessment. We know we need to improve and expand our systems, but at the same time we can't be getting every piece of software that gets released or is requested by an end user.

*Agenda:* Mr. Prospect, that's one of the things I would like to go over with you today. I would like to get a better understanding of what you are trying to accomplish with software and hardware applications and what your challenges are, and introduce to you what we have been doing in the area of software and hardware innovations.

*Gain interest:* Because of our expertise, we have been able to assist companies in identifying and selecting the right solutions for their application, while avoiding the common traps of buying software or hardware that will not be utilized fully.

This is what I would like to cover today. Is there anything you would like to add or change?

*Client response:* No, that sounds fine.

*Objective:* If all goes well, and I can get the information I need, I would like to schedule an appointment with you and others involved in the decision to be able to submit a proposal in about a week.

But I have to repeat what my friend Mike McNeill says: "This is the only profession where people go out and actually practice in front of their customers. They like to get into a sales call, let it flow, and end up wherever it takes them." You have to rehearse your timing repeatedly, at least until you feel comfortable with the process and preferably before every call.

Finally, I began the preface of this book by saying, "I am a salesman." I've been, I am, out there. When I was younger, I read how-to books and said about many of them, "This is the pie-in-the-sky. This is not the way it works in the real world." That's a trap I hope I'm avoiding here; I recognize that there's no such thing as a textbook sales call. I understand also that you can follow every step I've suggested, spend hours at the library researching your prospect and his or her company, create a common ground the size of Alaska, and the prospect will still come up with a way to throw you off your rhythm.

The sad (and obvious) fact is that you will not close every sale. Based on the surveys I do, out of every one hundred sales calls, about 20 percent are calls you'll close. Another 30 percent will go to the competition. But fully 50 percent won't buy from you no matter what you do! You have a limited amount of time available to you. A sales call, and the preparation for it, not only eats into that precious resource, but it's an expensive out-of-pocket cost for your company as well.

## Action Steps to Qualify Your Prospects

That's why I make a point of trying to qualify prospects by first asking them to take an action step—that is to do something that doesn't necessarily take a lot of effort, yet indicates a level of interest. In my case, I'll ask a prospect to fill out a brief questionnaire. When I get a completed questionnaire back, I not only know that I have a real shot at a sale here, but I also have the answers the prospect has provided me with. This means I can walk into a meeting armed with more information than I would have otherwise.

For example, in one day I received two calls about the SDI training course. The first one came from a sales executive at a Philadelphia software company who said he'd seen an advertisement I'd run in a local business magazine and was wondering if I could send him more information. A short time later, I received a call from a large Cleveland company. The person who called said, "We *want* you to do a training program for us." The caller didn't say, "We're *thinking* about having you run a program for us." He said, "We *want* you to run a program for us." That's a potential buying signal, something we'll discuss in the upcoming chapter.

I sent both callers brief questionnaires. A week or so went by, and I hadn't heard from either of them. So I called the Cleveland company, the one where I was sure I had a sale. The executive said, "Oh, yeah, we'll get to it; we'll get to it." On the other hand, when I called the software company, the sales executive said, "Gee, I hope you don't mind. But we've photo-copied your questionnaire and distributed it to our sales force. We're in the process of tabulating their responses now." My question to you is which company do you think is a better pros-pect? Where do you think I made the sale?

How you qualify a customer depends upon a variety of factors, including your industry. You don't have to ask a pros-pect to fill out a questionnaire. However, the questionnaire I use is shown in Figure 3-1.

As you can see, the questionnaire is designed so that filling it out doesn't take a lot of effort. Remember, an action step doesn't have to be difficult to be effective.

If you believe that constructing a questionnaire is too dif-ficult or that filling one out is too much to ask of prospects, then ask them to send you something simple, for example, an annual report, a set of drawings, or a list of people involved in a specific project.

If they respond, take that as an action step; it's an indica-tion that there is at least a modicum of interest, a level of seriousness that makes the prospect worth pursuing. Over a six-month period, we at SDI analyzed what happened to the questionnaires that we had mailed out. Approximately 37 per-cent of the questionnaires were returned, completely filled out. Another 8 percent were sent back, but were incomplete with some questions not answered. Others were answered only incompletely. Finally, over half, 55 percent, were not returned at all.

When we compared the response ratio to the closing ratio, there were absolutely no surprises. When we called on people who had filled out the questionnaires completely, we were able to close a sale 89 percent of the time. Of those prospects whose responses were haphazard, we were able to close only 30 per-

**Figure 3-1.** SDI survey.

*SDI*

*Sell With Commitment*

Please complete the following survey and fax your responses to
(215)449-3910 to receive your sales survey report and direction for
achieving increased sales excellence.

Please complete all areas indicated by a →

→   **To:**    Sales Development Institute

**From:** Name: _____ Phone _____

Company _____ Title _____

Product/Service sold _____ # of Salespeople _____

Address _____

State _____ Zip _____

→    1. Based on the performance and observation of your sales force, please rate their current level of abilities in the
categories listed below:

|  | very good at this | average at this | need to improve at this |
|---|---|---|---|
| • Preparing and planning for a sales call. Establishing and achieving goals. | ❏ | ❏ | ❏ |
| • Creating strategic account development plans. | ❏ | ❏ | ❏ |
| • Asking better questions to understand the motives, needs, thought processes of the prospect. | ❏ | ❏ | ❏ |
| • Listening skills. | ❏ | ❏ | ❏ |
| • Presenting solutions through benefits, features, and advantages. | ❏ | ❏ | ❏ |
| • Positioning of your product/service. | ❏ | ❏ | ❏ |
| • Solving problems. | ❏ | ❏ | ❏ |
| • Resolving objections, obstacles, and minimizing resistance. | ❏ | ❏ | ❏ |
| • Differentiating company from the competition. | ❏ | ❏ | ❏ |
| • Replacing the incumbent supplier. | ❏ | ❏ | ❏ |

|  | very good at this | average at this | need to improve at this |
|---|---|---|---|
| • Developing consultative/partnering relationships with prospect. | ☐ | ☐ | ☐ |
| • Identifying the personalities of prospect and adapting to their buying and communication style. | ☐ | ☐ | ☐ |
| • Getting the price you want. Establishing value in your service. | ☐ | ☐ | ☐ |
| • Gaining commitment—implementing closing as a process. | ☐ | ☐ | ☐ |
| • Productivity, time, and territory management. | ☐ | ☐ | ☐ |
| • Effective business writing. | ☐ | ☐ | ☐ |
| • Influencing and persuading the prospect. | ☐ | ☐ | ☐ |
| • Negotiating. | ☐ | ☐ | ☐ |
| • Using the telephone to arrange appointments and as a sales tool. | ☐ | ☐ | ☐ |
| • Prospecting and developing a market plan. | ☐ | ☐ | ☐ |

→ 2. As a result of completing this survey, please identify at least three areas that need improvement.

_____

_____

_____

→ 3. What do you see as the major challenges and issues in developing new business, increasing sales, and maintaining customers?

_____

_____

_____

**Thank you for completing the survey.**
**Please fax your responses to us now at (215) 449-3910**

*"Past success doesn't guarantee future performance, only the constant drive for knowledge, refinement, and persistence will."*
–CHARLES D. BRENNAN, SDI

cent of the time. Finally, when we followed up on people who hadn't completed their questionnaires, we were able to make a sale only 15 percent of the time.

## Some More About Action Steps

Action steps are an easy way to qualify how serious a prospect is about your product or service, but they can do more than that. It's perfectly all right to ask a prospect to take one at any point in the quarter-half-quarter model. In addition to the questionnaire, here are some other action steps prospects can take to show just how serious they are:

- Give you their Federal Express number so that they are billed when you send overnight material to them.
- Write a memo to other decision makers about your service or product.
- Attend a meeting at your office.
- Call your references.
- Pay for a sample or attend a seminar.
- Provide a list of decision makers along with their addresses and phone numbers.
- Provide confidential information or documents.
- Share a cost for a presentation or activity, for example, rent a meeting room in a hotel or pay expenses for your trip to a branch office.
- Meet with you during off-hours.
- Offer you a home phone number.
- Participate in a site tour.
- Prepare drawings.
- Sign up for a small order or agree to a prototype.
- Provide personal introduction to top executives.
- Provide needed resources to move the sales process along.
- Write your product into order specifications.

As you can see, there are a wide range of possible action steps. The ones that fit you and your sales cycle best will depend largely on your industry. As a rule, I try to get a prospect to commit to at least one action step on each sales call.

Action steps are clear indications of interest. But sometimes even the best salespeople are thrown off the scent by statements they misunderstand or misinterpret. They believe, or they want to believe, that the customer is on the verge of signing a contract, when, in fact, the prospect is hardly interested at all. For example, when the Cleveland company said, "We want you . . . ," I perceived that to be a buying signal when it really wasn't. In addition, the intent of action steps is also to balance the inequities surrounding the sales process. Consider that the average sales call costs close to $300 (according to McGraw-Hill), submitting a proposal can range from a few hundred dollars to thousands, and there is time and effort, as well as expense, in preparation and travel. With those costs in mind, it isn't asking much for a prospect to take a few minutes to do something for you.

Figuring out what is and what isn't a buying signal and how to respond will be discussed in the next chapter.

# Chapter 4

## *Listening, Selling Yourself, and Selling Change*

Good salespeople recognize the importance of understanding their clients and their clients' needs. Getting information about your clients' operation—what's working, what isn't—is essential if you're going to develop the type of relationship that separates you from the competition.

The best way to get the information you need is to use a skill that not many people cultivate anymore and that is to listen with an attuned ear. I'm sure all of us can recall instances in our own lives where people may have *listened* to what we were saying, but they didn't *hear* what we said. More often than not, they heard what they wanted to hear.

We're all guilty of this in our everyday lives, and if you don't believe me, ask your spouse or your companion. But the problem is that when we mishear during a sales call and misinterpret a signal a client sends us, we run the risk of moving too quickly and advancing directly to the presentation quarter of our quarter-half-quarter model when we still need to be building the relationship.

Remember, when we discussed the adjectives used to describe our friends in Chapter 1, we recognized that building that kind of relationship takes time. The same holds true for a sales relationship. As with a friendship, rushing can only sour your association.

Whenever I'm on a sales call, I frequently do more than listen. I ask permission to take notes. I consider my initial visit with a prospect as much an interview as it is sales call. During a call I'm not just a salesman or just a consultant, I'm also a reporter. And like a journalist, I ask questions. If I'm asking the right questions and getting the proper responses, I'll be getting the kind of information I can use to help build this relationship.

This data is too important to trust to memory, at least my memory. And, frankly, I've found that if I do nothing but take notes, that alone sets me apart. More than one client has told me that one of the things they remember about the first time we met was that I pulled out a long legal pad and took down almost everything they said. But taking notes down and comprehending the significance of what you're being told are two different things. The most difficult task of all is recognizing a prospect's level of interest.

## Hearing, But Not Always Believing

The difficulty goes beyond what I alluded to earlier. It's not just a matter that you hear what you want to, by that I mean you *listen* to an essentially noncommittal comment, but you *hear* a very positive statement. Another problem is that most people, especially prospects, it seems, don't like to be the bearer of sad tidings. So they'll couch even negative news in the most positive terms or just delay telling you the bad news (and not take your calls) in the hope that you'll go away. It's called "masking," and we all do it.

Instead of simply saying, "No, No. A thousand times, no!" (or words to that effect), they fudge. They say, "Sounds good." or "Let's talk about your idea next week." It's important to learn how to categorize these statements and even the accompanying body language to determine a prospect's level of interest. There are essentially three possibilities:

1. *Negative.* Indicates complete disinterest, skepticism, and/or resistance
2. *Noncommittal.* An impartial attitude toward you, your product, idea, service or solution
3. *Positive.* Displays supportive, encouraging, or optimistic position where an intent of action is present

Listed below are some of the most common verbal and physical responses you get from prospects. Using the definitions of interest listed above, take a second to define the statements and actions in Figure 4-1. Now compare your answers to the most common responses from approximately 3,000 participants in the SDI program in Figure 4-2. Finally, compare your answers to the correct responses in Figure 4-3.

As you can see, there's often a wide discrepancy between perception and reality. But, again, that's understandable. From the time we get into sales, we gear ourselves to pick up on buying signals. As a result, sometimes when we hear something that's even close, we misinterpret it.

Consider a common question prospects often ask, "What's your product availability?" At first glance, that seems positive.

**Figure 4-1.** Categorizing prospect's responses.

| | N | NC | P |
|---|---|---|---|
| 1. "Call me next week. I need time to prepare your proposal against two others." | ☐ | ☐ | ☐ |
| 2. Prospect leans towards you. | ☐ | ☐ | ☐ |
| 3. Prospect expresses concern about past dealings with your company. | ☐ | ☐ | ☐ |
| 4. "Sounds good. Leave your literature—I'll look it over." | ☐ | ☐ | ☐ |
| 5. "We could have used this last year. This will work well with our operation." | ☐ | ☐ | ☐ |
| 6. "I like it, but it's not in our budget." | ☐ | ☐ | ☐ |
| 7. "What's your availability?" | ☐ | ☐ | ☐ |
| 8. "I need to get approval from my manager." | ☐ | ☐ | ☐ |
| 9. "That was a great presentation." | ☐ | ☐ | ☐ |

**Figure 4-2.** Common prospect responses in SDI program.

| | N | NC | P |
|---|---|---|---|
| 1. "Call me next week. I need time to prepare your proposal against two others." | ☐ | ☑ | ☐ |
| 2. Prospect leans towards you. | ☐ | ☐ | ☑ |
| 3. Prospect expresses concern about past dealings with your company. | ☑ | ☐ | ☐ |
| 4. "Sounds good. Leave your literature—I'll look it over." | ☐ | ☐ | ☑ |
| 5. "We could have used this last year. This will work well with our operation." | ☐ | ☐ | ☑ |
| 6. "I like it, but it's not in our budget." | ☐ | ☑ | ☐ |
| 7. "What's your availability?" | ☐ | ☐ | ☑ |
| 8. "I need to get approval from my manager." | ☐ | ☑ | ☐ |
| 9. "That was a great presentation." | ☐ | ☐ | ☑ |

You may very well think it's a step forward in your relationship with the client, virtually a commitment. But of course it isn't, because as soon as you leave, the prospect is as likely to call one of your competitors to find out about product availability there as he or she is to place an order with you.

At the conclusion of a recent presentation I made to a major automotive manufacturer, I was escorted to my car by the company's vice president of training who had chaired the meeting. He told me, "That was probably the most outstanding presentation I've ever seen." And I knew immediately that I had lost the deal. For while his comment was very positive, he, nevertheless, remained very noncommittal. If he felt my presentation was really that good, he would have suggested further action such as, "I'm going to send you a contract."; "I'll

**Figure 4-3.** Correct prospect responses.

| | N | NC | P |
|---|---|---|---|
| 1. "Call me next week. I need time to prepare your proposal against two others." | ☐ | ☑ | ☐ |
| 2. Prospect leans towards you. | ☐ | ☑ | ☐ |
| 3. Prospect expresses concern about past dealings with your company. | ☑ | ☐ | ☐ |
| 4. "Sounds good. Leave your literature—I'll look it over." | ☐ | ☑ | ☐ |
| 5. "We could have used this last year. This will work well with our operation." | ☐ | ☐ | ☑ |
| 6. "I like it, but it's not in our budget." | ☐ | ☑ | ☐ |
| 7. "What's your availability?" | ☐ | ☑ | ☐ |
| 8. "I need to get approval from my manager." | ☐ | ☑ | ☐ |
| 9. "That was a great presentation." | ☐ | ☑ | ☐ |

recommend you to my directors."; or, "Here's what I want you to do." You have to be aware of these hidden signals.

However, you may wonder, "Couldn't he merely have meant what he said, that the presentation was great? Perhaps he had no hidden agenda." You may be correct but not in this particular case. I did not get the contract. Yes, sometimes people make simple statements that must be accepted at face value. And that's fine in your regular life, your *real* life, so to speak.

For example, I love Indy car racing. When I was dating my wife, I'd suggest we go at every opportunity, and she always said, "Sounds good." We've been married over ten years now. I still ask her about going to the races, and she still says, "Sounds good." But I've learned that "Sounds good" doesn't mean go out and get tickets. Rather it means let me know the date and I'll schedule something else for us.

## What You Should Be Selling

Making this discovery in my personal life only cost me the price of two admission tickets some years ago. But making the same mistake in a business situation could cost you a deal. It's very easy to misinterpret, "Sounds good."

But that's your job as a salesperson. In fact, it goes deeper than that. There are just so many hours in a working day. If you're going to spend them most productively, it means concentrating on your best opportunities. Ideally, then, not only do you have to categorize a prospect's level of commitment, you also ought to be able to determine his or her receptiveness to change.

I always ask the participants to tell me the three things they sell, and I'd like you to list them now too.

1. _____
2. _____
3. _____

Typically, the responses I receive are:

1. Myself
2. My product
3. My solution

These responses are not wrong, but they're not entirely right either. Answers number two and three, the product and solution, are really the same and should be the last thing you sell. Yes, you should sell yourself and, by extension, the relationship with your client. But you also have to sell the recognition that there's a need for change. I used a medical analogy before to illustrate a point; this time I'll move to the dental field.

Imagine you're on the road, and you develop a toothache. You ask a colleague or the hotel desk clerk to recommend a local dentist or maybe you just look up dentists in the phone book. You call for an appointment, tell the receptionist it's an emergency, and it is your good fortune that the dentist has an opening and can fit you in right away.

When you get there, are you going to ask the dentist what dental school he or she went to? Or what grades this person earned in school? Or even how much is this going to cost? No, you're not. You are in pain. You want change. And if you see anything that even resembles a dental license, you'll allow this dentist to work on your tooth.

This is exactly the same situation you want your prospects to be in: pain. Figurative pain, anyway. You want them not only to recognize the need for change, you also want them to be grateful to you for showing up and offering them a solution.

## The Three Levels of Client Interest

When it comes to receptiveness to change, most prospects fall into one of three categories or levels of interest: opportunity, need, and change. See Figure 4-4.

**Figure 4-4.** Categories of client's interest.

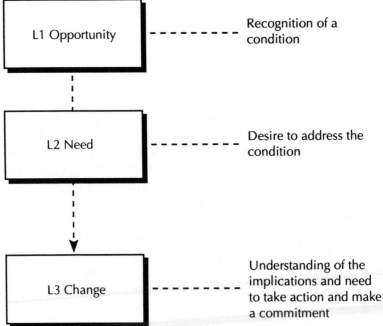

*Level One: Opportunity.* This is when a prospect indicates that there is an area or areas in which your product or service might provide a solution. When a prospect makes a statement that is opportunistic, it usually lacks a clear statement of desire to correct the situation at hand.

> *For example*: We have been thinking about talking to a company that specializes in state and local taxes.
> *Or*: We've been considering adding assembly line robots for some time now.

*Level Two: Need.* A prospect expresses a desire that can be met by your product or service. Because it represents a desire, it is far more positive than an opportunity. But it differs from change because it lacks a commitment to take action.

> *For example*: We have been thinking about talking to a com-

**Figure 4-5.** Prospect's receptivity to change statements.

| | L-1 | L-2 | L-3 |
|---|---|---|---|
| 1. "Call me next week. I need time to prepare your proposal against two others." | ☐ | ☐ | ☐ |
| 2. Prospect leans towards you. | ☐ | ☐ | ☐ |
| 3. Prospect expresses concern about past dealings with your company. | ☐ | ☐ | ☐ |
| 4. "Sounds good. Leave your literature—I'll look it over." | ☐ | ☐ | ☐ |
| 5. "We could have used this last year. This will work well with our operation." | ☐ | ☐ | ☐ |
| 6. "I like it, but it's not in our budget." | ☐ | ☐ | ☐ |
| 7. "What's your availability?" | ☐ | ☐ | ☐ |
| 8. "I need to get approval from my manager." | ☐ | ☐ | ☐ |
| 9. "That was a great presentation." | ☐ | ☐ | ☐ |

pany that specializes in state and local taxes because of our growing concern in this area.

*Or*: We've been considering adding assembly line robots because we hear our competition is planning to.

*Level Three: Recognition of change.* A prospect indicates an understanding of the implications of continuing present actions and not making the change.

*For example*: We have been thinking about talking to a company that specializes in state and local taxes because of our growing concern in that area and because of the possibility of losing hundreds of thousands of dollars.

*Or*: We've been considering adding assembly line robots because we hear our competition is planning to do so, and we could lose market share as a result.

**Figure 4-6.** Correct receptivity to change statements.

| | L-1 | L-2 | L-3 |
|---|---|---|---|
| 1. "Call me next week. I need time to prepare your proposal against two others." | ☑ | ☐ | ☐ |
| 2. Prospect leans towards you. | ☑ | ☐ | ☐ |
| 3. Prospect expresses concern about past dealings with your company. | ☑ | ☐ | ☐ |
| 4. "Sounds good. Leave your literature—I'll look it over." | ☑ | ☐ | ☐ |
| 5. "We could have used this last year. This will work well with our operation." | ☐ | ☑ | ☐ |
| 6. "I like it, but it's not in our budget." | ☑ | ☐ | ☐ |
| 7. "What's your availability?" | ☑ | ☐ | ☐ |
| 8. "I need to get approval from my manager." | ☑ | ☐ | ☐ |
| 9. "That was a great presentation." | ☑ | ☐ | ☐ |

In the same way that you earlier categorized a prospect's level of interest, you should now analyze the same statements in order to determine a prospect's receptivity to change in Figure 4-5. Now take a look at the correct answers in Figure 4-6.

Obviously, you're not going to get a lot of Level Three recognitions of change. Studies at SDI show that 70 percent of the statements clients make during the first sales call fall in the Level One or *opportunity* category. Only 25 percent of prospects make statements at Level Two which indicates some kind of *need* for change. The remainder, 5 percent, recognize the importance of change, but usually only when something is broken.

As a salesperson, you have to recognize the different levels of the buying mode and be able to move your client up to Level Three. Now comes the fun part, where we start talking about dialogue and asking the right questions that at once build a relationship and convince the prospect that he has a toothache.

# Chapter 5

## *Building the Foundation for Dialogue*

There are several basic principles of the quarter-half-quarter approach to selling I've developed, and one of the most important is worth repeating: Your goal is to raise your prospects' awareness of the fact that they are in pain, that they must find a way to change the way they are currently conducting business in order to relieve that pain, and that your solution, whether it's a product or a service, is the best possible medicine.

How are you going to do that? Hopefully, one point I've established well is that the wrong approach is to *tell* the prospect that he or she must change. Again, using words is the least effective way to make a point. When you resort to doing that, you're working at a 93 percent failure rate.

The correct approach is to involve prospects in the kind of dialogue that gets them thinking about the ways they conduct their business and ways that process might be improved. This is simple, you say? Certainly, almost by definition, salespeople are gregarious folks, super people able to start conversations faster than a speeding bullet and able to tell tall stories in a single bound. All right, I'm not going to beat this metaphor to death, but I'm sure you get the idea.

The problem is that sometimes salespeople are too gregarious. The sales manager for a filter distribution company constantly complains to me that his salespeople, as well as salespeople who call on him, talk too much. They don't give prospects an opportunity to engage in a dialogue with them, even if the prospect wants to. Typically, he says, a sales call is dominated by the *salesperson's* monologues, opinions, and presentations. As a result, since the prospect isn't given an opportunity to recognize his or her pain through dialogue with the salesperson, the call will be a failure.

But success isn't certain even when salespeople allow prospects to enter the conversation because just having a regular conversation isn't sufficient enough to accomplish your objectives. The fact is that there is a substantial difference between just making conversation, like you might at a cocktail party, and making *meaningful* conversations. By meaningful conversations, I mean those that create *meaningful* dialogue, provide you with *meaningful* information, and, finally, set you apart from the salespeople who come in, make idle chatter, and dominate any discussion.

How do you best involve someone in a meaningful conversation? Think about it for a minute. Do you have any ideas? Right, the easiest way to involve someone in a conversation is to ask him or her a question. Don't you agree?

Questions elicit responses. They provide you with the information that you need to move the sales cycle along. They create a dialogue, and they create a relationship. Typically when I make these points someone will get up and say, "I ask questions all the time." Yes, all salespeople ask questions. But, more often than not, salespeople don't ask enough questions or the right kind of questions, and they don't spend enough time, as noted in the last chapter, listening to the responses.

To illustrate my point, I'd like you to take just five minutes and write down ten questions that you typically ask prospects on the telephone or during a first or second sales call. At this point, certainly, I'm not looking for your ten *best* questions. Just the first ten that come to mind.

1. _____
2. _____
3. _____
4. _____
5. _____
6. _____
7. _____

8.  _____
9.  _____
10. _____

Usually when I do this exercise with a group of salespeople, most participants think it is going to be a snap. They start off with a great deal of confidence, but no more than three minutes into the exercise, some of the people who were the cockiest start to squirm.

If you didn't come up with ten questions, don't worry. Very few people do. In fact, the average at one of my seminars is most often somewhere between six and seven questions. In a study I conducted, 87 percent of the 3,000 salespeople surveyed said yes, they knew the importance of asking questions. But only 27 percent, slightly more than a quarter, were then able to demonstrate the ability to ask well thought out questions that would stimulate dialogue.

It became clear to me quite early on that most salespeople need to make significant improvement in asking questions that generate dialogue. What do I mean by that? Essentially, there are two types of questions you can ask your prospect. The first provokes a recitation response; the second results in a dialogue.

A recitation response is one in which the prospect answers with something he or she already knows by rote. Typical recitation-provoking questions include:

- How many manufacturing facilities do you have?
- Where are they?
- What are your goals?
- Who are your current vendors?

There is nothing wrong with a recitation-provoking question. Very often they elicit important information that you need, to provide the prospect with a meaningful solution, and they are a necessary ingredient of every sales call. But a prospect providing a recitation response is simply giving you information he or she already knows. There's no thought involved and no real opportunity to move into new directions.

Beyond that, recitation responses are very often available from sources other than your prospect. If I were a prospect, I'd have serious reservations about a potential vendor who took up my time asking me how many plants my company has, where they are, and who my current suppliers are. So do a little homework and answer these questions yourself!

Moreover, asking those kinds of questions is the same as opening the conversation by marveling at the stuffed swordfish I have mounted behind my desk. Everyone who comes in will have asked me the same thing.

On the other hand, a dialogue-provoking question often requires complex thinking on the part of the prospect. Because this type of question often solicits an opinion rather than just a correct answer, it usually involves longer exchanges among individuals. Also in a dialogue type of conversation, the prospect or buyer will contribute at least 70 percent to the conversation. Compare that figure with the consultative selling diagram in Figure 1-2 which suggests that 70 percent of the focus ought to be on the buyer.

Some dialogue-provoking questions are:

- Describe your biggest challenge. How does it compare to last year's?
- Describe for me the effects of the economic recovery on your planning efforts. How have they influenced your thought process compared to a year ago?
- Explain the selection process of a new vendor at your company. How does it compare to industry standards?
- Could you please describe the circumstances and the course of events that led to the current condition?

As you can see, these questions aren't designed simply to get an answer. Their intent is to make the prospect think and to open avenues for a discussion. Once you get a discussion going and the prospect thinking, rather than reciting, the potential benefits are numerous; they will help you achieve several of your goals, such as gaining more information, differentiating yourself from the competition, and moving the sales process along.

One of the most obvious benefits is that prospects will look at you differently. I cannot tell you how many times I'm on a sales call and the prospect will say, "You know, no one has ever asked me that before." The prospect will look at you differently from the way he looks at the "how many manufacturing plants do you have" salesperson. You will have created a meaningful difference. And chances are you will have earned some respect as well as taken the first important step to building a long-term relationship.

As important is the fact that the prospect has come to the sales call with a certain set of expectations. You will try to sell to him or her and he or she will try to maintain the status quo. But by creating a dialogue, literally forcing the prospect to think and perhaps look at something from a different perspective, you raise the possibility of change. You will know that you have a shot at success if the prospect says, "You know, I never looked at it that way."

Finally, dialogue creates a sense of intimacy and trust. And once you accomplish that, you've bridged the gap from an anonymous salesperson to a salesperson with a relationship. And as I've discussed previously, surveys of buyers indicate that their relationship with the salesperson is one of the key factors in the buy/don't buy decision-making process.

Now that you understand the importance of creating an atmosphere of dialogue, I'll begin to discuss the art of asking questions and how to build those skills as well as the different types of questions and when to ask them. Mastering these skills is at the very heart of the process that will transform you from just a good salesperson to a super salesperson.

# Chapter 6

## *The Barbara Walters Rules*

There is one television show I never miss. No matter where I am or what I'm doing (within reason, of course), I drop everything when one of Barbara Walters's specials airs. Even if you don't watch them, chances are you've probably heard about them. They're usually an hour long and divided into three or four segments, each an interview with a currently hot celebrity. Usually, but not always, the celebrity is involved in the entertainment industry, but other high-profile individuals, including politicians have also been interviewed.

Invariably, these shows generate a lot of publicity because Barbara almost always gets at least one of her guests to either make a startling statement, confront some previously hidden aspect of his or her past, or just cry. The sportscaster Frank Gifford and his wife, talk show host Kathie Lee Gifford, taped a segment with Barbara, and the week after it aired, Frank's *Monday Night Football* colleagues were kidding him about his interview, to which Frank replied, "I can't believe I said what I did."

At the risk of sounding silly, I admit that hearing Frank's comment was an important moment for me because it crystallized the essence of what I teach. If I could capture and bottle it, I'd give it to each of you because what happened to Frank, what prompted him to say that, is hopefully what we're doing as salespeople and is what our questioning techniques can prompt our clients to say.

## Adapting Barbara Walters's Technique to Your Sales Calls

We ought to be getting people so involved with us, so relaxed and so trusting, that they converse with us not as business associates, but as they would with a friend. However, you may believe that there is no relationship between what Barbara Walters does and what you do in your sales calls, but that's not true. What she did with the Giffords, what she typically does with everyone she interviews, is use many of the techniques I've discussed in the preceding chapters and will elaborate on in future chapters.

First of all, she asks questions to engage her guests and get them involved in conversation. Second, she asks the right kinds of questions. You won't hear her interrogate her guests. She doesn't ask a lot of questions that allow for recitation responses. Instead, she is really good at asking questions that generate dialogue, questions that make people think. Also she listens. In fact, she really follows the consultative approach where, 70 percent of the time she's listening and learning. But the analogy between Barbara Walters and your sales calls goes beyond the questions she asks. There are also similarities between the celebrities she interviews and the prospects you call on.

Typically, celebrities go out on tour to promote their latest project—a film, a television show, or a book. They'll travel around the country doing four or five, or even more, interviews a day, answering the same questions over and over and over again. Just a few days or so into a promotional tour, the celebrities know what questions they're going to be asked, the probable order in which they'll be asked, and the answers that are expected to them. For example:

*Interviewer*: Isn't this role different from any you've attempted before?
*Celebrity*: Why yes it is, but I feel it's important that I stretch as an actor.

*Interviewer*: This book is different from anything you've written before, isn't it?

*Celebrity*: Why yes it is, but I feel it's important that I stretch as an author.

Well, the same is likely to be true about your prospect. The chances are excellent that many salespeople start a conversation by commenting on the fish on the prospect's wall and asking about the number of manufacturing plants he or she has, or about the company's goals. It isn't long before a prospect can literally make a sales call on him or herself.

Again, you have several important goals, and all of these can be achieved if you become sales versions of Barbara Walters.

• First, and I cannot stress this enough, in an era where products and pricing tend to be similar, if not the same, clients say they buy relationships. Therefore, you want to make yourself stand apart from the crowd and to position yourself as a unique factor in the equation. How do you do that? By asking different questions that show you are a salesperson who has done his or her homework, who is intelligent and who has put some thought into the sales call process.

• Second, you want to create a dialogue with your prospect. How do you do that? Like Barbara Walters, you create dialogue by asking the right kinds of questions, questions that engage prospects in meaningful conversation.

• Third, you want to create an atmosphere for change, and yes, you can do that also, with the right kinds of questions. One of Barbara Walters's most famous questions is, "If you were a tree (or a flower or an animal), what kind of tree would you be?" On the face of it, that's a pretty silly question. However, because it is so different, so unexpected, her guests can't give her an automatic "just like every other interview" kind of answer. They have to stop and think. They have to look at this interview differently from what they had anticipated before it began. They have to *change*.

Obviously, I'm not suggesting that you ask your prospects what kinds of trees they'd be. But clearly, in a business context, asking questions that make prospects think and examine their methods of operation in a different light can be a significant benefit.

In the next few pages, we're going to discuss what I call the "Barbara Walters Rules of Conduct and Good Questions." I'm also going to offer a list of characteristics of what makes a good question. And finally I'll discuss a few different kinds of questions and how best to utilize them.

## Barbara Walters's Rules of Conduct

In Chapter 1, I discussed how a UCLA survey shows that you are judged less by what you say as how you say it. I also suggested that it is important to properly read the prospect's non-verbal messages. It's important to remember as well that the prospect is watching you too and is trying to read what you say and how you say it. So, before you even attempt to formulate good questions, look at the following guidelines for questioning. Most are just common sense, but they still are broken all too frequently:

- *After you ask a question, be quiet.* As nature abhors a vacuum, salespeople abhor silence. Though it may not be in your character, allow the prospect time to think about an answer. If your question is good, no additional comment is necessary.

- *Ask the question once.* This is not too difficult. Still, you'd be surprised at how many salespeople have been embarrassed to have a prospect say, "You just asked me that," when they have inadvertently repeated a question. More often than not, it's simply a function of nervousness. Sometimes, we're so busy trying to concoct another question, we lose track of where we've been. I generally have several questions written down in advance, and I put a check mark by each as I ask it. Simple problem. Simple solution.

- *When speaking to more than one person, address questions to everyone.* In a group sales call, I think we all have a tendency to concentrate our attention on the person we perceive to be the decision maker. This is not a good idea for a variety of reasons. First of all, we could be wrong. The person we think is the decision maker may not be. Or it may genuinely be a group decision. Or the person who is ignored and not a decision maker today, may be promoted tomorrow. Beyond that, focusing attention on just one person is impolite. All those are good reasons, but the most important of all is that you want the burden of thought to fall on everyone. Ideally, you want everyone engaged in the conversation, everyone becoming aware of the need for change.

- *Listen to what's being said. Do not think of your next question.* It's easy to let your attention wander and to leapfrog to the next question you want to ask in order to stay ahead of the prospect. But while your motives may be good, letting your mind stray for whatever reason is dangerous. While you're worrying about the next question, the prospect may be saying something important or asking you a question. What do you say then? "I'm sorry. I wasn't paying attention." I know it's ridiculous for me to even have to mention this rule, but I've often seen it not happen.

- *Be prepared with additional questions.* This may sound like it's the opposite of what I've just said, but it isn't. I always walk in with at least three, and often as many as five, questions. Clients are almost always concerned with a number of issues, such as: cost containment, productivity, profitability, quality of the work force and the product. You should be prepared with questions on each of these issues, or the issues of your client, in so far as your product or service can resolve the client's concerns about them. For example, if your product or service won't have an impact on the quality of the work force, then that's not an issue you need to address.

Often, I don't ask all of my questions because a prospect's answers or comments send me off in a different direction from the one I'd planned to go in. This is another reason to pay attention to what the prospect is saying. But it's still important to have additional questions ready and not only to address the client's issues. These questions can serve as a kind of insurance policy—insurance that we don't hit that part of a sales call that all salespeople detest, the dreaded lull in conversation. Conversational lulls tend to lead to recitation-provoking questions that serve little purpose, as I discussed in the last chapter.

- *If appropriate, acknowledge the main points the prospect makes by requesting more information.* It's okay to say that you find something the prospect has said fascinating and ask him or her for more data. Or you may request clarification if the prospect says something you don't understand. In either case, it shows you've been listening and that tends to be interpreted as a positive sign.

- *Try to create a neutral environment.* There are subtle, and sometimes not so subtle, issues of comfort and control involved with every sales call. People are very comfortable in their own offices, but you as salespeople are not in control in your prospect's territory. The office is his or her haven. He or she can choose to accept or not to accept telephone calls or to be either distracted or not distracted by other visitors. If possible, and I know it isn't always, try to create a neutral environment in which to meet a client. Suggest the call take place in a conference room. Movement works. For example, former Presidents Reagan and Gorbachev, apparently hit a lull while negotiating the arms agreement in Iceland. President Reagan suggested the two go out for a walk, and the change in location made all the difference in the world. They reached an accord during their walk.

- *Be clear and concise.* At times salespeople will use techniques that require lengthy questions. But no matter how long they are, the questions must be clear and easily understood. For example, one of the biggest mistakes salespeople make is that they ask the same question twice. It's not that they repeat a question, but as they ask a question, they rephrase it as they ask it. For example, I have actually heard salespeople ask, "How is it that you've managed to maintain your sales in a down market? By that I mean, everyone else's sales are down, but yours are just about the same, if not a little higher, than last year's?" This may be an extreme example, but this kind of question happens all the time. It makes you look silly and unprepared. On the other hand, if you have a good question and it isn't answered, or at least answered properly, ask it again and rephrase it then if you need to.

- *Know what ideas you want to develop as you compose your questions.* Just as you have a goal for every sales call, you ought to have a goal for every question. Whenever I follow up with people who have taken the SDI course, I discover that some graduates become super-converts to the "asking questions to build understanding" philosophy. The problem is that though they may ask dialogue-provoking questions, the dialogue they provoke isn't always relevant to the sales call. If you're selling widgets, the questions you ask must generate dialogue about widgets, not the economy, politics, or computers.

It is said that a good lawyer never asks a witness a question he or she doesn't already know the answer to. Well, the same is true for salespeople. You have to ask yourself: What am I going to learn when I hear the answer? Will the response be something that allows me to continue the conversation, or will it lead me to a dead end? If you learn something helpful or if the response continues you on the path of the sale, then the question is a good one.

Another example of what I call *misdirection*, is when a salesperson asks a question that forces a prospect to focus on how *good* things are going, rather than on the pain he or she is experiencing—pain that can only be alleviated by change. A typical scenario goes something like this:

> **Salesperson**: How are things going with your current supplier?
> **Prospect**: Good, we're very happy.
> **Salesperson**: Why? What is it doing right?

On the surface, the question makes sense. You want to find out as much as you can about the prospect's views and relationship with his or her present vendors. But stop and think what you've just done. Your question has actually forced the prospect to focus attention on what your competitor is doing correctly.

- *Using emotion is good, if it's done properly.* Asking people how they feel about something can be an effective tool, but it can also be dangerous and should be used with some care. On the plus side, asking someone's views is flattering and provides him or her with part ownership of the conversation. However, if the subject is one that your prospect is uncomfortable with—for example, the prospect indicates that things aren't going as well as planned—then your asking, "How do you feel about that?" will likely get you a response that's agitated, emotionally charged, and counterproductive to what you want to accomplish. A small point here: If you're attempting to build a relationship that is based on emotion, then remember when you want to get a person's opinion, ask the person how he *feels* (which is based on emotion) not what he *thinks* (which is based on logic).

- *Finally, and this is very important, don't get discouraged!* This material is the basis of a course I give hundreds of times a year. Whenever I get to this point, I sense restlessness, and I understand why.

I've just thrown a number of rules at you, and there will be more in the next few chapters. The temptation, no doubt, is to say, "This is too much. I'll never master these rules." DON'T GIVE IN TO TEMPTATION!

First of all, if you look back at these rules, you'll see that many of them are simply common sense. There are some rules and techniques I've listed that you probably already use. Mastering the rest is simply a matter of time. I see this happen in my course when I conduct role-playing scenarios and written exercises. The person who said, "Practice makes perfect" was right.

By the end of the course, the participants have improved their questioning skills. Almost always, the improvement is dramatic. Sometimes, though, it's just a bit. But everyone gets better, and, as our follow-up surveys show, they continue to improve to the degree that they utilize all these skills. Even Barbara Walters didn't ask great questions at first.

One significant factor that works in your favor is that most people genuinely want to share information. They have egos, and given the opportunity, enjoy talking about themselves and what they do. Moreover, we've become increasingly isolated as a society—communicating by electronic mail, along computer networks, by fax, or by cellular phone. Chances are your prospect is primed to talk face-to-face. All you need to do is to get him or her started.

In the next several chapters, we're going to discuss the different types of questions to ask, and how to formulate them.

# Chapter 7

## *Formulating the Right Kinds of Questions*

Jim McAlea, who has become a friend of mine, is vice president of Waco Associates, a Philadelphia-based filters and pumps company. He is also a firm believer in the consultative selling approach and regularly sends his students through the SDI program.

Before he signed on with SDI, he'd handled training for Waco's sixteen person sales force himself. But, he says, "I wanted to create a different image of an industrial sales force. I also thought my sales weren't going up at the rate they should." He felt he needed an outside trainer to get his sales effort up to snuff and, as I understand it, asked approximately fifty sales trainers to fill out a questionnaire. "Only about five came back completed," McAlea recalls. "I was surprised at the unprofessionalism of some of these people."

I find it ironic that in this case it was the *buyer* who asked for an action step, but I went along with it. We met and discussed his situation. At the time, his salespeople weren't using good questioning techniques. He apparently liked what I had to say, and I gave a seminar to his employees.

"What I liked about Charlie's approach is that he has structured the questioning techniques in such a way that whether you're a seasoned salesperson or a newcomer, they're easy to adopt and will enhance your success," McAlea says. He adds, "Right now we have a professional consultative selling team, and I don't use that term lightly. Also, we've had significant growth in sales and profits."

I offer this endorsement here because I believe it is important that you recognize that the questioning techniques I'm going to introduce over the next few pages work. They are, as my friend Jim McAlea says, *structured*. By that he means there isn't a great deal of guesswork involved. It's laid out for you much like a road map. Because it is so structured, the technique is *easy to adopt*, not only to the sales cycle of any industry or service, but by salespeople at any level of experience. You will be able to build relationships with prospects that will lead to a *significant growth in sales and profits*.

## Closed Probe Questions

Most people familiar with consultative selling have already been introduced to the concept of open and closed probes. Probing is just another way of saying questioning, and the idea behind it involves gathering information and discovering a client's needs.

There are two kinds of probing questions: open probes and closed probes. Closed probes limit the range of a client's responses to yes or no answers as well as a limited range of answers based on the alternatives you supply.

A closed probe question is likely to begin with words like: *do, does, is, are, have, has, which,* or *or*. They might begin questions such as:

- Are you looking for a way to eliminate that problem?
- Do you handle more than ten jobs a day?
- Which of these problems most affects your operation?

The kind of answers you can expect from closed probe questions like these are: *Of course. No.* and *The first.*

As you no doubt can see, it is likely that these kinds of responses, which are typical of what you get when you ask a closed probe question, will be short and to the point. They are not apt to move you closer to your goal of starting a meaningful conversation. You will use closed probes when you want a specific commitment from a prospect, at the end of each phase of the sales call or the quarter-half-quarter model, for instance, but they should not be at the heart of your call.

## Open Probe Questions

An open probe, on the other hand, encourages a lengthier reply. Open probe questions are likely to begin with words like: *who, when, where, why, tell me, how,* and *what.* Some examples include:

- What are your goals for this year?
- When did you begin to notice the problem?
- Where did it begin?
- How has the system been working?

As you can see, the responses that these questions are likely to provoke are longer.

Probing questions are the cornerstone of the consultative selling process, but I don't think open and closed probes go far enough. The reason is that both open and closed probe questions as currently understood and practiced still typically call for recitation responses such as:

- My goal this year is for a 15 percent increase in sales.
- The problem began to manifest itself last year, just before the spring selling season.
- The problem began with a glitch in the fuel injection system.
- The new system is working out just fine.

Remember, you have several goals on this sales call. First, recognizing that there are probably few product or price differences between you and your competitors, you want to establish the relationship as a significant factor in the decision-making process. You want to do that also because you know that surveys show that the relationship between salesperson and client is often the most important factor of that process.

We do that by asking questions, the right kinds of questions: dialogue-probing questions that get prospects to look at their situation in a new light, questions that get prospects to recognize that they have a problem, questions that get prospects to recognize their pain as well as their need for change to alleviate that pain, and of course, your prescription as the best and most viable solution.

This is not to say that you should totally eliminate open and closed probe questions. In point of fact, they are still useful. For example, every time you exit one section of your quarter-half-quarter model, you should ask a closed probe question that gets your prospect to confirm that you're moving closer to your goal:

- If all goes well, is it possible to arrange a meeting with the other members of your committee?
- Are you available to spend a day at our production facility?

## A New Definition for Your Questions

As mentioned earlier, open and closed probes almost always call for recitation responses. So if we hope to build a relationship with our prospects and to understand their positions and situations in order to precipitate change, and if we recognize that the easiest way to do that is through questioning, then we have to go beyond probe questions.

What I've done is redefine the traditional consultative selling questions. I've created four types of questions—informational, dialogue-probing, multi-layered-probing, and countering. Each has a distinct purpose and place in a sales call. And each is designed to help you fulfill your goals: getting the necessary information you need, building a relationship with the prospect by creating a dialogue and setting yourself apart from your competition because of your intelligence and perceptiveness.

## Informational Questions

I don't suppose it would surprise you if I said that informational questions are intended to get important data about the prospect's company. These questions typically resemble closed probes because they seek facts, figures, and details. They also build a foundation of intelligence from which to work.

Nevertheless, while informational questions can be useful in the sales process, they are easily misused and overused. First of all, informational questions don't set you apart from the competition. Informational questions—Where are your other plants located? or How many widgets do you order each quarter?—are likely to be asked by everyone on every sales call. Informational questions will not set you apart from other salespeople.

Second, salespeople frequently use informational questions in lieu of doing research. However, even though prospects like to be helpful, they resent doing your work for you.

Third, answers to informational questions are always recitation responses. Also, they tend to deal with peripheral issues. Therefore, they don't lead to the kinds of meaningful conversations that lead to the discovery of pain and consequent change.

Finally, informational questions are asked to assist the seller, not the buyer. There is nothing in them for the prospect.

That's not to say that informational questions don't serve any purpose at all. For one thing, they enable you to get intelligence that might not be available elsewhere. For example, if you're calling on a privately held company that doesn't have an annual report, informational questions provide access to details you need to have if you're going to come up with intelligent solutions.

Very often, also, informational questions are the equivalent of an athlete warming up before a game. A few informational questions at the beginning of a sales call is one easy and effective way to get a conversation started. Remember not to misuse or overuse them. I try to keep it at a ratio of two informational questions to one dialogue-provoking question.

## Common Questions

Based on SDI surveys, what follows are several questions commonly asked by salespeople at some point in the sales cycle:

- Do you make the final decision?
- Do you have money in the budget?
- What are your goals?
- Where does your company want to be six months from now?
- Who is your best vendor and why?
- Is there anything I can do to help close?
- What is the area you would most like to improve?
- Can I supply you with a proposal?
- How many relocations are there annually?
- What are your plans for changes in benefits?
- What are your clients' investment needs?
- Is your competition experiencing growth?

If you're in the real estate business, I don't suppose you're going to ask about clients' investment needs, and conversely, I suspect financial advisers are relatively unconcerned about the number of employees a company relocates. But I'll bet there are numerous questions on this list that you have asked. And looking back at them now, I'm sure you'll see that all these questions, even those peculiar to a specific industry, have a number of things in common.

The first is that they all call for recitation responses. The prospect pretty much has all the required information at his or her fingertips. There's no special thought process involved. And while the information you learn may be valuable, these questions don't fit any of the criteria I've established as important. Recognizing that this information is still important, you can place your recitation-provoking questions on a questionnaire and forward them to your prospect for completion. This serves as an action step and helps avoid your asking these questions on the sales call. Recitation-provoking questions don't engage people in conversation, and they don't differentiate you from the dozens of other salespeople who call on the prospect.

## Dialogue-Probing Questions

If you should not use informational questions, what should you be using? At the heart of the sales call, you ought to use dialogue-probing questions, which are everything that informational recitation-provoking questions are not. As you will see, dialogue-probing questions stimulate complex thinking, ultimately get a prospect to look at his situation in a different way and, as a result, make him or her more susceptible to change. These are not questions that allow recitation or simple yes or no answers.

And, most important, *dialogue-probing questions create complex thinking by creating comparisons.* So, for example, you don't ask a prospect, "How do you make a purchasing decision?" You ask instead, Has the economy had any impact on the way you make purchasing decisions compared to the way you made them, say, ten years ago?

## What Dialogue-Probing Questions Can Do

*Point one.* The differences in the way you word a question can have a significant impact on the type of response you receive. Consider version one: "How do you make a purchasing decision?" If I were the prospect, I believe my initial reaction to that question would be, "Hey none of your business!" But by phrasing it in a dialogue-probing manner, the effect will be different. For one thing, you're no longer giving the appearance of being nosy. To refresh your memory, refer to the examples of such questions in Chapter 6.

*Point two.* The prospect will very likely have to stop and think. This will not be a typical recitation response.

*Point three.* Because the question itself is interesting, you are likely not only to get a response, but an honest response. More to the point, not only will you learn how purchasing decisions are made, the entire process will be put in perspective for you.

*Point four.* You will stand apart. The prospect has probably never heard the question phrased that way, so you are automatically put in a category by yourself.

*Point five.* You have engaged the prospect, and you are now involved in a dialogue. Also you are now en route to creating an environment in which change is possible, and the prospect can recognize his or her pain as well as discover a way to get rid of it.

*Point six.* Phrasing the question as a dialogue-probing question by asking for a comparison with the way the decision-making process was conducted a decade ago requires more than just a simple thought process. By adding an element of time and how time has had an impact on a situation, you're forcing the prospect into an in-depth thought process that requires him or her to put occasionally complex matters into some kind of perspective.

## The Sales Process Made Easy

And the best part of all, this process is really simple. It does not require the wholesale revamping of a sales organization or your sales process. But I don't want to oversimplify the process, either. It demands that you accept the consultative approach to selling. You must recognize that good sales calls are properly paced, and I've given you an easy-to-follow model for achieving the correct sales tempo. Finally, you have to understand that good questions are properly formatted. But as you can see, the formatting is easy. It is just a matter of taking a standard probing question and adding a comparative phrase to it.

An easy way to do that is by creating a chronological comparison. That is, you don't want to know how your prospects make purchasing decisions. Rather you want to know how the way they make purchasing decisions today are different from the way they made them a year or two ago.

But comparisons do not always have to be centered on

time. In some cases, that may be impossible. And even if it is possible, a continuous stream of time-related dialogue-probing questions can become boring or even irritating. However, comparisons can also be created by comparing the prospect company's practices to industry trends, accepted procedures, or documented positions taken by industry spokespeople. For example, "Describe for me the impact that the trend towards just-in-time delivery has made on your purchasing decision."

## Turning Probing Questions Into Dialogue-Probing Questions

Let's take the common questions I discussed before and turn them into dialogue-probing questions. These are not necessarily bad questions, but they are asked by everyone using almost exactly the same phrasing to the point that prospects can answer the questions in their sleep. As worded, these questions do not break prospects out of their current thinking patterns or paradigms, and they don't induce change.

Bernie Weidenauer, a director of sales at ARCO Chemical, always says to me, "What we're after is getting that one nugget of information that no one else has." What a different approach to questioning does is break the pattern, break the paradigm, and open the prospect up to new ways of thinking and to giving you that needed nugget of information.

- Do you make the final decision?
- Do you have money in the budget?
- What are your goals?
- Where does your company want to be six months from now?
- Who is your best vendor and why?
- Is there anything I can do to help close?
- What is the area you would most like to improve?
- Can I supply you with a proposal?
- How many relocations are there annually?
- What are your plans for changes in benefits?

- What are your clients' investment needs?
- Is your competition experiencing growth?

## Changing Common Questions to
## Dialogue-Probing Questions

There really is no right or wrong question here, but here are the ways I would have asked these questions:

- Do you make the final decision?
- ☑ Describe for me the selection process of a vendor and how this compares to the way you handled this process in the past.

- Do you have money in the budget?
- ☑ Tell me the budget process you go through in this area and how that compares with other areas you fund.

- What are your goals?
- ☑ Describe for me your goals and how they compare to your thoughts and plans in the past.

- Where does your company want to be six months from now?
- ☑ Explain the path your company is going to take in the next six months and the factors that will lead you in that direction.

- Who is your best vendor and why?
- ☑ Tell me the criteria you have for this product or service and how that compares to existing conditions.

- Is there anything I can do to help close?
- ☑ Share with me the role a vendor plays in assisting you in the buying process and how that compares to other departments?

- What is the area you would most like to improve?
- ☑ Explore with me the areas you would most like to improve and the reasons that you identify these issues over others.

- Can I supply you with a proposal?
☑ Tell me the criteria you look for in a proposal and what you think might happen if I successfully meet them.

- How many relocations are there annually?
☑ Share with me the number of relocations you experience annually and how this compares to trends of years past.

- What are your plans for changes in benefits?
☑ Explore with me the present conditions of your benefit program and how this area has matured and changed over the last several years.

- What are your clients' investment needs?
☑ Describe for me the requirements your clients look for in terms of their investments and how these have changed over the last five years.

- Is your competition experiencing growth?
☑ Looking at your competition, what have you noticed in their growth, and what do you believe has prompted this expansion?

## Some Dialogue-Probing Tips

Your questions probably aren't the same as mine, but I'll bet that they're close enough. Almost inevitably when I do this exercise in a seminar, the students are surprised at how simple formulating these questions is, certainly a great deal easier than it looks. It is just a matter of practice and getting used to doing it. Remember, though it may seem easy to formulate these questions, they're still important because they may set the tone for the entire meeting. If you impress the prospect right at the start, the entire sales process will flow, easily.

There are a few tips that may make the process easier. I noted that one easy way to come up with a good dialogue-probing question is by creating a chronological comparison. That is, you're asking the prospect to put his present situation in terms of the past (what brought the company to its present situation), in terms of the present (comparing the company's situation to others in the marketplace), or in terms of the future (where the company plans to go).

Look at the time line below:

| | | |
|---|---|---|
| **Past** | **Present** | **Future** |

About 90 percent of the questions we ask are formulated in the present or the future. Rarely do they address the past. You may very well say, what's past is past and has no relevance for the present. But that's not true. As Shakespeare said in *The Tempest*, "What's past is prologue." To understand the present or the future, you have to first understand the past. In fact, that is so axiomatic, it is almost always the way we learn things in school. We're almost always taught about a country or a people or even a subject by first learning its history.

In sports, teams study their opponents' tendencies. They prepare by studying their opponents' habits and how they react under game conditions. They hope that viewing their opponents' previous games will reveal what they might do in the future.

Consider that a large part of understanding chemistry begins with the alchemists of centuries ago. It's hard to understand psychology without first coming to grips with Freud. It's easier to understand the political process if we recognize that it's an outgrowth of the British parliamentary system. I could go on and on. There is an endless supply of examples of what I mean. But certainly the message is clear.

When you ask a basic question such as, "What are your goals?" you're going from the present to the future. But you are leaving out an important, perhaps the most important, piece of the pie: The past. Almost everyone fails to ask about the course of events that led to the present and that shaped the thinking process that determined future goals. Once we understand this, why the client is taking a particular approach and why it is traveling in a specific direction, the easier it is for us as salespeople to identify the prospect's pain, create a need to change, and present the solution.

So whenever possible attempt to frame a chronological comparison in terms of the prospect's history. It's not always possible, and even if it is possible, it's not always wise to use this approach. But a series of properly framed chronological comparisons that delve into a prospect company's history will help you understand your mission far better.

Another factor is that whatever comparison you use, you have to frame the question in a nonthreatening manner. For example, if you say *"The Wall Street Journal* recently ran an article that said good managers are empowering their people with a combination of challenge, security, and reward. How does this compare to what you're doing?"*, the manner in which this question is worded can suggest that your prospect is handling his employees differently from top managers. That's probably not what you meant, but you can see that the implication is there. Think how you would respond if you were asked the question that way. At the very least, you'd probably be a little bit defensive. And chances are you'd also be a little angry, though you may not show it, which obviously is not an emotion a salesperson wants to encourage in a prospect.

Finally, it's been my experience that you're far better off abandoning the traditional *who, what, when, where, why* approach to your questioning. As already noted, starting off questions with any of the traditional five "w"s tends to lead to recitation responses. On the other hand, using descriptive words *explain, describe, explore* or phrases like "all things being equal," "share with me," "walk me through," "in the event of," "course of events that led . . ." will challenge your prospect to listen, absorb your question, and respond. Remember, it's not the complexity of what you ask that determines what kind of response you get but the intelligence of what you ask.

## Practice Makes Perfect

Although it varies from class to class and from industry to industry, a certain percentage of participants in my seminars feel uncomfortable with these questions. Part of that is a general uneasiness with doing things differently. To that I say, if you feel uneasy about changing something as simple as the way you ask a question, imagine how your prospect feels about changing a supplier. So the first step is to improve your receptiveness to change. *Do you, are you, will you* questions easily roll off our tongues. But as soon as you see the results, *explain, explore, investigate* questions will become a regular part of your arsenal.

# Chapter 8

## *Multi-Layered-Probing Questions*

Michael Ludwig is regional sales manager for W. W. Grainger, Chicago, the nation's largest distributor of industrial supplies and equipment. He is currently based in Dallas; in his previous assignment, he was the company's district sales manager for Philadelphia and eastern Pennsylvania. When he arrived there, that district rated ninth out of ten in the company—until he generated one of the strongest sales increases in the region. Ludwig tells how:

"The consultative selling approach we adopted is much more sophisticated than what we did in the past. We'd just give customers our catalog and throw in a 10 percent off promotion. What the Sales Development Institute did for us was help us make the transition from selling the product to selling the services we provide that accompany the product.

"He [the author] did that with some of his work on probing, how to ask the right kind of questions that really get to the heart of a customer's problems so that we could offer solutions. Once we learned that, we started to see results inside of six months."

Mike Ludwig isn't alone. Jim Still, sales director of Softmart, an Exton, Pennsylvania-based reseller of PC-based business software, peripherals, and networks, put his twenty-five-person sales force through my course. He says:

"The most effective part of the course, I thought, was using questions to get to a customer's pain. The questioning approach to selling is based on customers' needs and takes you away from telling and selling. Before the course, we were kind of playing it by ear. We had nothing that was really structured. We weren't asking the right questions. Often, we weren't asking any questions, period. Or if we were asking them, they were questions that elicited a 'yes' or 'no' response, questions that really didn't get you anywhere. After our people went through the course, they began to ask questions that led customers down the road to their actual needs and to recognizing the need for change. And it got customers talking more about what they do and what their company does."

I quote Ludwig and Still to reinforce the central theme of this book: my belief that asking the right kinds of questions is the easiest technique to enable salespeople to both better understand their clients' needs and build a stronger relationship with them. But, as with anything new, it invariably takes some getting used to.

Typically, when I get to this point in my seminars, about half the participants are converts ready to buy into my theory. With role-playing exercises, they see how good question-asking skills can improve their performance. While it's difficult to qualify, I almost always get the sense that it isn't that the other 50 percent of the class doesn't agree with the theory per se. It's just that they seem to have problems coming to grips with all the different kinds of questions: recitation, dialogue-probing, informational.

"Do I need a Ph.D. in questionology?" a salesperson asked during one of my sessions. I knew where he was coming from. It seems complicated in the same way a piano seems complicated to someone who has never taken a lesson or an engine seems complicated to someone who isn't a mechanic. But the ability to play a piano and to tune an engine are *learned* skills, and once you learn them, they unlock the mysteries of engines and pianos which aren't that complicated after all.

It is the same with good sales questioning techniques. I believe that when it comes to questions, as with everything else in life, there are no absolutes, just shades of gray. Different kinds of questions elicit different kinds of answers in different circumstances. And as you practice these skills, what seems complex turns out not to be so intricate.

Finally, I want to point out an article that ran in *The New York Times* as I was writing this book. The article compared the results of a survey conducted by a national political candidate (where the questions obviously were biased in favor of the candidate) with the results of an independent pollster who used the same questions, phrased more neutrally.

The point of the article was that survey results can easily be manipulated, depending upon the way a question is phrased and even who is doing the asking. That applies to good salesmanship also. The answer you get depends upon the way you ask the question. For example, when the candidate asked, "Should laws be passed to eliminate all possibilities of special interests giving huge sums of money to candidates," 99 percent of his respondents said "yes."

However, when an independent pollster asked the same question *with the same wording*, the results were different. Only 80 percent said "yes", 17 percent said "no", and 3 percent didn't know or didn't answer.

But when the professional pollster rephrased the same question *in a more neutral format*, the results were surprisingly different. The revised question was: "Should laws be passed to prohibit interest groups from contributing to campaigns, or do groups have a right to contribute to the candidates they support?" Now, only 40 percent were in favor of prohibiting group contributions while 55 percent of the respondents contended that groups have the right to make contributions!

It just proves my point. You are what you ask.

## Multi-Layered-Probing Questions

Having said that, I have to introduce another type of question. I call it a multi-layered-probing question or MLPQ. It is the most encompassing and, therefore, most important questioning technique you will learn. MLPQs have the same goal as dialogue-probing questions—that is, their purpose is to encourage complex thinking, as well as to get prospects to look at their operation differently, to recognize their pain, and, most important, to recognize the need for change.

But MLPQs are a little more sophisticated than straight di-alogue-probing questions, and they give you a kind of comfort zone that lets you delve into areas you might not otherwise be able to scrutinize. Let me explain. MLPQs have three parts:

1. A statement of fact
2. An observation, generally one supporting that fact
3. A dialogue-probing question

*The statement of fact.* This is simply a reference to some un-impeachable source, usually a respected publication. For ex-ample, you might say something like: "I just read an article in *The Wall Street Journal* that said housing starts are up this year over last year."

Starting your MLPQ this way achieves a number of objec-tives. First of all, it adds credibility to your question and, by a kind of osmosis, to you. Remember, though, while it is per-fectly acceptable to make reference to an article in *The Philadel-phia Inquirer*, talking about a recent report you read in the *National Enquirer*, even if you do have an inquring mind, is a no-no.

By using a fact gleaned from a respected source, it becomes virtually unchallengeable. Consider a television interview I saw a few years ago with real estate mogul, Donald Trump. He was, at the time, going through a number of personal and profes-sional difficulties, and, given his enormous debt load, there was considerable doubt over whether his empire would sur-vive. The interviewer asked him, "Common sense says that one of the best ways to reduce your debt is to sell assets. What as-sets are you likely to sell?"

On the face of it, there doesn't appear to be anything wrong with the question. Indeed, when you can't pay your bills, common sense does dictate that you sell assets. However, the interviewer was a noted television personality, who isn't recognized for her economic expertise. So her contention that selling assets is common sense while probably correct, is still arguable. Donald Trump, who has substantially more expertise in finance, could easily have said, "No, what is common sense is riding out this storm because the economy is going to improve."

Or: "No, what's common sense is bringing in a few investors while essentially retaining ownership of everything."

Or: "No, what's common sense is rearranging my debt with my banks."

Or, worse still: "No, what's common sense is ending this interview now." And, of course, when I say *interview,* that could just as easily be *sales call.*

The journalist would have been much better off had she begun her question something like this: "*Business Week* recently ran an article that said the best way to reduce debt is to sell assets." That would have added substantial validity to her statement. Also another advantage of starting off with a fact gleaned elsewhere is that if your prospect disagrees with it, he or she is attacking an article, an independent statement, not you or your company.

If, on the other hand, you start off with a statement about yourself or your product—such as, "Ninety-four percent of our customers are satisfied with our products," the disagreement, if there is any, can become personal.

Remember also that one of the major goals here is to get a dialogue going. If you load up your MLPQ with a statement about you or your product, the prospect may feel that he or she is being set up and will give a less than candid response.

*An observation, generally one supporting that fact.* The purpose here is to lend even further credibility to your statement. Going back to that *Wall Street Journal* article I mentioned earlier, you might follow up with, "The builders I've spoken to over the last month have told me they're experiencing substantial increases in sales." What this does is lend real-life believability to your opening statement, and it sets the prospect up for your dialogue-probing question.

*A dialogue-probing question.* This is the kind of question I discussed in the last chapter. In this case, the question might be: "If that is your experience as well, explore with me how you think this will affect buying habits compared to 1980, the last time building rebounded from a recession."

## Some MLPQ Tips

The most important thing to remember about this entire process, particularly when it comes to MLPQs, is that it is flexible. If I've learned anything in my years in sales, it's that if there is one hard-and-fast rule, it's that there are no absolutes.

For example, it's perfectly okay to flip-flop the statement of fact and observation and then ask your question. There are occasions, particularly later on in the sales cycle, when flip-flopping is preferable. But this is acceptable, at times, even on a first call. It really doesn't make a lot of difference if you phrase the MLPQ this way: "The builders I've been speaking to have told me that they've been experiencing substantial increases in sales. And I just read an article in *The Wall Street Journal* that says this is not just a local phenomenon. Builders around the country seem to be in better shape. If that is your experience as well, explore with me how you think this will affect buying habits compared to 1980, the last time building rebounded from a recession."

In fact, it's probably a good idea to switch the order in which you ask MLPQs on a regular basis, if just to change the pace of the questioning. You want to be prepared—preparation is the key to success—but you don't want to appear programmed. Unless you vary the pace of your questions, you stand the risk of having your entire presentation seem canned.

If every question has the same rhythm—Fact, Observation, Question; Fact, Observation, Question; Fact, Observation, Question—it becomes boring and makes it seem as though you are an overrehearsed actor rather than a sincere salesperson intent on building a long-term relationship.

■ *Read your questions out loud.* This is the most ignored piece of advice I've ever given. Why do you have to read questions out loud? Most people don't realize that the written word and spoken word are different. When we speak, we use contractions. Usually, when people write, they do not. When we speak, we tend to use simple words and phrases. When we write, we rarely use rudimentary expressions when hundred dollar words will do as well. When you reread your written questions, they'll sound perfectly all right. But if you speak the words, your ear will pick up any discrepancies. You'll recognize where you have written *cannot* when you would normally say *can't*. In addition, making the questions as conversational as possible is important. This will increase the prospect's receptivity and understanding.

■ *The observation doesn't always have to support the fact.* In the most common MLPQs, the observation and fact are in alignment: they support each other. And that type of arrangement works well. But there are other ways to compose MLPQs that can create the kind of attitude and conversation you want to generate. You can use what I call third party information or something that is not *directly* related to the fact. Here's an example.

During a role-playing exercise, I ask seminar participants to construct MLPQs, and, to make it easier, I suggest that they build them around some recent headlines. For instance, during the time a set of classes was under way a few years ago, New Jersey introduced a law prohibiting restaurants from serving runny eggs. The intent of the legislation was to halt the spread of salmonella poisoning spread by undercooked eggs, but the general consensus was that this law was unnecessary, a kind of silly way to achieve that goal. It was soon repealed but not before it became the subject of an interesting MLPQ. One participant phrased his MLPQ this way:

*The statement of fact was:* "The State of New Jersey has a law restricting the sale of undercooked eggs which have been linked to the spread of salmonella poisoning."

*The observation was:* "In the motion picture *Rocky*, Sylvester Stallone drinks six raw eggs for breakfast. The perception created for children is that this is a healthy practice."

*The dialogue-probing question was:* "In what way does this have an impact on or justify the runny egg law?"

I have said before that there is no right and wrong in constructing MLPQs. And if one of the goals of this form of question is to get someone to look at a problem or situation in a different way than they might have in the past, then this question is certainly on target. In fact, pairing two issues that probably haven't been coupled before stimulates interesting conversation. It intrigues listeners and creates a new dynamic to what may (for your prospect, anyway) be an old conversation.

However, these issues have to have some logical connection, some common thread. Sly Stallone and the runny egg law are just about as divergent a fact and observation as I feel comfortable with. It's okay to go from *A* to *T* to get to *C*. It's a long way, but it's doable. Going from *A* to *Z* to get to *C* is just a bit too much.

Another MLPQ approach is to take two diametrically opposed positions and ask a dialogue-probing question that asks the prospect to weigh both sides of a given situation. But, again, both positions must have a common thread. For example, in researching a company prior to making a sales call, I read their annual report which stated that a cornerstone of this company's corporate philosophy is to focus on the development and advancement of its people. Then I found an article in *The Philadelphia Inquirer* that seemed to indicate the opposite, that the company preferred to bring in executives from the outside.

When I saw the vice president of training, I asked, "Your annual report states a commitment to employee development. Yet an article I saw in *The Philadelphia Inquirer* suggested just the opposite. Can you describe for me your position on training and how that compares to the *Inquirer* article?"

This example illustrates several of the points I've made about MLPQs. You may have noticed that what I used here wasn't a fact and observation, but two facts. *You have to work with what you have.*

Second, the question created a safe environment for the prospect's response. I could have backed him into a corner by using the *Inquirer* article as the center of the MLPQ. Instead, I asked the prospect his opinion of that article and how that compared to his own experience. By positioning the facts that way, I created a harmless, protected atmosphere that allowed him to respond honestly and for me to get information that ultimately led to a sale.

One last example: Top economists are noticing a reduction

in customer spending; recent reports state the opposite. Describe your perspective and how it compares to the reports.

Finally, this is really simple. Believe me. I didn't realize exactly how simple this was until I was listening to a popular radio call-in talk show. A man who identified himself as a construction worker asked the host, "*Sports Illustrated* magazine called Philadelphia Eagles Quarterback Randall Cunningham 'the ultimate weapon.' But, in today's paper, some writer said he doesn't think Cunningham has the tools to elevate the team to the next level. With that in mind, how would you evaluate Randall's performance and which article is more accurate?"

Without any formal training, this man asked an MLPQ as naturally as if he'd been doing it all his life. This, of course, is my point. It is only a matter of time before dialogue-probing and multi-layered-probing questions flow from your lips naturally too. An MLPQ is a perfectly natural way to ask a question, as you will soon see.

## Some MLPQ Exercises

Do you remember the most commonly asked questions I introduced in earlier chapters. Here are several of them, again. To make things easier, I'll supply you with a fact and observation as well. Just complete the MLPQ with a good dialogue probe:

- Do you make the final decision?

*Fact:* *Purchasing* magazine recently reported that General Motors is instituting a vendor reduction program in the hopes of saving a billion dollars in costs.

*Observation:* Other companies I've spoken to seem to be changing the way they select vendors too.

*Dialogue probe:* _____

_____

- Do you have money in the budget?

*Fact:* In today's environment, developing a budget and then staying within it was one of the top three concerns expressed by managers in a recent survey by *The Wall Street Journal*.

*Observation:* Many of the managers I've discussed this with agree that the proper allocation of funds is critical but so is walking the fine line between letting the numbers overwhelm them and doing what's necessary to grow their departments.

*Dialogue probe:* _____

_____

_____

- What are your goals?

*Fact: Computer Age* magazine recently wrote about the difficulty many MIS managers are facing in planning because of all the rapid advancements that are taking place in technology.

*Observation:* A number of the managers I've spoken to are undecided about whether to act now or wait for the next version to come along.

*Dialogue probe:* _____

_____

_____

- What are your challenges?

*Fact:* An article in *Fortune* magazine pointed out that the advent of fiber optics, microwave communications, and the growth of cable and LAN networks has greatly increased the number of choices available when corporations select communications systems.

*Observation:* These elements have created a race among industry leaders to be the first and best in their areas of specialization.

*Dialogue probe:* _____

_____

_____

Please take a moment to complete the above exercise.

## Some Recommended Answers

Each MLPQ could have had any one of several dialogue probes. They vary depending upon the salesperson, the prospect, and the situation. Here's the way I answered the questions:

- Do you make the final decision?

*Fact: Purchasing* magazine recently reported that General Motors is instituting a vendor reduction program in the hopes of saving a billion dollars in costs.

*Observation:* Other companies I've spoken to seem to be changing the way they select vendors too.

*Dialogue probe: Share with me your selection process. Does it compare to trends in the industry, and how did you handle the process several years ago?*

- Do you have money in the budget?

*Fact:* In today's environment, developing a budget and then staying within it was one of the top three concerns expressed by managers in a recent survey by *The Wall Street Journal.*

*Observation:* Many of the managers I've discussed this with agree that the proper allocation of funds is critical but so is walking the fine line between letting the numbers overwhelm them and doing what's necessary to grow their departments.

*Dialogue probe: Describe for me the budget process you go through and what you're doing differently now than you did ten years ago.*

- What are your goals?

*Fact: Computer Age* magazine recently wrote about the difficulty many MIS managers are facing in planning because of all the rapid advancements that are taking place in technology.

*Observation:* A number of the managers I've spoken to are undecided about whether to act now or wait for the next version to come along.

*Dialogue probe: Keeping in mind this quick technological obsolescence, can you describe your MIS goals and how they compare with your thoughts and plans in the past?*

- What are your challenges?

*Fact:* An article in *Fortune* magazine pointed out that the advent of fiber optics, microwave communications, and the growth of cable and LAN networks has greatly increased the number of choices available when corporations select communications systems.

*Observation:* These elements have created a race among industry leaders to be the first and best in their areas of specialization.

*Dialogue probe: Tell me about how these new technologies have affected your company and how your decisions regarding networking and communications have changed over the last five years.*

## An Exercise to Build MLPQ Muscles

I am almost willing to bet that your responses are not substantially different from mine. This process really is simple. What I'd like you to try now is a few MLPQs in which I supply you with the fact, and you fill in both the observation and dialogue probe.

• How do you decide which medications you prescribe (asked of a doctor by a pharmaceutical rep)?

*Fact: The Philadelphia Inquirer just ran an article about the dependence of doctors on people like me to provide them with the most up-to-date information about advances in medicines and technologies.*

*Observation:* _____

_____

_____

*Dialogue probe:* _____

_____

_____

• Where does your company want to be six months from now?

*Fact: It's hard to pick up a newspaper and not read a story about another large company reducing its staff and cutting costs.*

*Observation:* _____

_____

_____

*Dialogue probe:* _____

_____

_____

• Who else is involved in the decision-making process?

*Fact:* Because of the increasing need for knowledge in specialized areas such as taxes, compliance, and audits, the decision-making process in numerous mid- to large-size companies like yours has grown to include many individuals.

*Observation:* _____

_____

_____

*Dialogue probe:* _____

_____

_____

Please take a moment to complete the above exercise.

Here are some possible answers. Remember, there is no single *correct* response.

• How do you decide which medications you prescribe (asked of a doctor by a pharmaceutical rep)?

*Fact: The Philadelphia Inquirer* just ran an article about the dependence of doctors on people like me to provide them with the most up-to-date information about advances in medicines and technologies.

*Observation:* Some industry critics claim that the demands placed on some physicians today don't allow them sufficient time to conduct their own research.

*Dialogue probe:* Explore with me the conditions present in your practice and how this has changed over the last few years.

• Where does your company want to be six months from now?

*Fact:* It's hard to pick up a newspaper and not read a story about another large company reducing its staff and cutting costs.

*Observation:* In an attempt to downsize, many companies are making their bottom line more attractive for the short-term, but they are possibly jeopardizing the future.

*Dialogue probe:* Explain the path your company is going to take over the next six months. What are the factors that led you in this direction and how does it compare to previous projections and industry trends?

- Who else is involved in the decision-making process?

*Fact:* Because of the increasing need for knowledge in specialized areas such as taxes, compliance, and audits, the decision-making process in numerous mid- to large-size companies like yours has grown to include many individuals.

*Observation:* There doesn't appear to be a set pattern that companies follow in selecting a new vendor or how many people are involved in the decision.

*Dialogue probe:* Share with me how the selection process occurs in your company and how it has changed over the years.

## Testing Your Questioning Expertise

By now if you are typical of salespeople in my classes, most of you now recognize how simple the system is. Also I'm willing to bet that you've absorbed far more than you realize.

So far, we've discussed three kinds of questions: informational, dialogue-probing and multi-layered. Each of the following questions falls into one of those three categories. Identify them either as informational (I), dialogue-probing (DP), or multi-layered (MLPQ).

_____ What's your budget for this project?

_____ Describe the circumstances and course of events that led to the current condition.

_____ Recent surveys indicate a need to improve performance. This was supported by several leading business experts. Can you describe your company's position on enhancing productivity and how that has changed over the last five years?

_____ Describe your biggest challenge.

_____ Describe your biggest challenge and how it compares to other industry leaders.

_____ I've been getting a lot of calls on the proposed tax legislation because of the concern about its effects on the manufacturing industry. Many people feel it will have a negative impact on the industry. Describe for me your company's view and how previous tax legislation has had an impact on your industry.

_____ Top economists have noted a dramatic reduction in customer spending. Recent reports issued by the federal government indicate the opposite. Can you describe for me what your experience has been?

_____ Who is your current vendor?

_____ Explain the process of selecting a new vendor at your company and how it compares to the manner in which new vendors were selected in the past.

Please take a moment to complete the above exercise.

Again, I'll bet that I didn't have to give the answers here. But I'll give them anyway:

__I__ What's your budget for this project?

__DP__ Describe the circumstances and course of events that led to the current condition.

__MLPQ__ Recent surveys indicate a need to improve performance. This was supported by several leading business experts. Can you describe your company's position on enhancing productivity and how that has changed over the last five years?

__I__ Describe your biggest challenge.

__DP__ Describe your biggest challenge and how it compares to other industry leaders.

__MLPQ__ I've been getting a lot of calls on the proposed tax legislation because of the concern about its effects on the manufacturing industry. Many people feel it will have a negative impact on the industry. Describe for me your company's view and how previous tax legislation has had an impact on your industry.

__MLPQ__ Top economists have noted a dramatic reduction in customer spending. Recent reports issued by the federal government indicate the opposite. Can you describe for me what your experience has been?

__I__ Who is your current vendor?

__DP__ Explain the process of selecting a new vendor at your company and how it compares to the manner in which new vendors were selected in the past.

Just one last note: In the second question, the first key word is *describe*, but another useful phrase to get the prospect to reflect back on the past is *course of events that led to the current condition*. This phrase will be useful in many applications.

Now let's put these techniques into action and learn how to funnel a prospect through the various levels from opportunity to change.

# Chapter 9

## *Funneling From Opportunity to Sale*

Throughout this book, I've kept hitting you over the head with several points I consider key to better salesmanship, my version of the recruiting commercial for the U.S. Army: Be all that you can be; sell all that you can sell. To achieve that goal, I've pointed out a few steps you'll have to take. You've got to:

- Adopt the quarter-half-quarter timing methodology, which allows you to control the sales call within the framework of the consultative selling approach
- Position yourself as the customer's partner and, in the process, build a relationship with him or her that differentiates you from the "I'm only interested in closing" salesperson
- Ask the right kinds of questions, questions that engage prospects in dialogue, allow them to recognize their need to change some phase of their operation, and position you as the person with the best solution to alleviating that pain

The way we perform that last task is a process I call funneling. See Figure 9-1.

Essentially funneling consists of linking a series of questions on a single topic. These questions engage the prospect in an in-depth dialogue and push him or her to disclose information and generate a willingness to change. Funneling allows

**Figure 9-1.** Funneling.

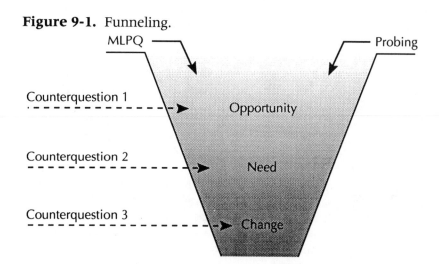

you to distinguish yourself from the competition because you have a better understanding of the prospect's condition. The application of the funneling process cements a relationship and creates an atmosphere of trust, agreement, and complete disclosure. But the art of funneling is dependent on more than just the questions you ask. As important is your ability to listen, to notice the fabric and feel of the discussion, and to recognize the emotion involved.

Typically, you go to a sales call with four funnels in mind—that is, four areas of concern to the prospect company. These are all situations you want to explore in depth. If you are successful, you will get information you need to close a sale and to help you expose a client's need to change. You have a good idea of what areas these are because you've done your research. Also, you select four funnels because as you go down one, perhaps even two, you may discover that what you thought was a problem is in fact a nonissue.

It's important to note, also, that you *must keep the funnels pure.* This is not the time or the place to make a sales pitch. The purpose of the funnel is to understand what prospects are thinking, how they got to where they are, and now that they're there, what they want to do.

## A Funneling Scenario

In the example that follows, the sales representative works for a large employment agency, and the rep wants to convince his client to use his company's services. You'll note that the rep starts off with an MLPQ:

*Sales rep:* You mentioned that you were going outside your organization to bring in expertise. In fact, I noticed in last month's issue of *Business Journal,* that you'd placed a help-wanted advertisement looking for computer programmers. What's the response been and how does that compare to your expectations?

*Prospect:* It's amazing. The number of responses we've received has been enormous, even greater than we expected. Unfortunately, the quality of the people applying for the positions has not been up to the level we anticipated.

*Sales rep:* You used the word *amazing* to describe the response. What made you select that word?

*Prospect:* What would you call it? That one advertisement generated over 600 responses.

*Sales rep:* I'll bet that was some chore going through all those résumés.Did the personnel department have to provide some staff members for that job, or did you handle it in MIS?

*Prospect:* We both pitched in. I had no idea how much time it would take to look through all those résumés and then interview qualified applicants. In retrospect, I can tell you that it was much more time-consuming than it was worth.

*Sales rep:* In what way was it more trouble than it was worth?

*Prospect:* We were expecting to find more people who were better qualified in the information systems we use. We were quite surprised at the number of people out there who applied for the jobs even though they are not proficient in our software and hardware.

*Sales rep:* If the situation remains unchanged, if you continue to have difficulty finding qualified people to fill these programming slots, what will be the impact on your department?

*Prospect:* It will slow our efforts and therefore slow our growth. This is definitely a problem we have to resolve because if we don't get conditions cleared up in the next thirty days we feel our service and response to customers will be downgraded. That will leave us with unsatisfied customers internally and externally. And it will probably mean that we'll also receive a poor evaluation on our ability to meet standards.

The questions the sales rep followed up with are called *countering* questions. They are intended to move the prospect further along down the funnel. While the opening MLPQ or dialogue-probing question in the funnel can be broad, *ensuing countering questions should be more specific, each getting the prospect to focus more on a specific problem.*

As you can see in the scenario above, the prospect came to recognize that placing a help-wanted ad, sifting through the stacks of résumés the ad generated, and then interviewing the best qualified respondents was not the best way to use his resources. Worse, it was potentially damaging to his company and his department.

## Closing a Funnel

There's no easy guidepost to tell you when you are near the bottom of the funnel. But, almost always, when you sense the prospect recognizes the need for change, you should ask, "What is the impact on the situation if nothing changes?" This question reveals whether the prospect recognizes that there is a need for change from existing practices.

For example, in the above example, when the impact question was asked it was revealed that customer satisfaction and performance, and perhaps even the prospect's own job security, were in jeopardy if the situation wasn't improved. When the person has revealed the consequences of nonaction, you have successfully reached the bottom of the funnel. *You are successful when the prospect has acknowledged the need for change.*

However, do not make the mistake of attempting to close a sale on someone at the bottom of the funnel. It is essential that you do not beat someone over the head with this newly acquired information. An example of this in the above scenario would be the sales rep saying something like: "If we can correct your hiring problem, will you engage us to find you programmers?

You don't want to force the issue at this point for two reasons. First, pushing to close the sale is the traditional approach, not the consultative approach that is the sign of a good salesperson. Second, most important, you still have to go down more funnels. If you close here, you will undoubtedly miss key issues that have not yet been disclosed in just one funnel. Also, although you may have made a sale, you will not have a relationship and you have probably missed other potential and lucrative business opportunities.

When you get the prospect to recognize the need for change, *move on to the next funnel.* Keep in mind that each funnel represents an issue of concern for the prospect. It might, for example, have to do with how the spiraling costs of health care are affecting your prospect's personnel costs with your goal being to get him or her to recognize the efficacy of temporary personnel. Or the next MLPQ might have to do with rising operational costs, funneling down to the prospect's recognition that there is a more cost efficient way to handle the problem.

Once you've finished funneling, you can now summarize all the pain or change issues that you've captured and ask your prospect if he or she is now ready to take steps to change. In your next breath, you can move into the fourth quarter (presentation of your solution).

As you can see, starting the funnel is *not* difficult. If you've done your research, there should be at least several reasons why your product or service will ease a prospect's pain. If you haven't done research to qualify the prospect, then all you're doing is making a cold call, and chances are, you're wasting everyone's time. And time is money.

If you have done your research and can't find four funnels, then this isn't a qualified prospect. It really doesn't make any sense at all to waste your time on companies that don't need to change, companies for whom your product or service doesn't fill a large void. Fortunately, every salesperson worth his or her salt knows the world is full of qualified prospects for whom you will easily be able to start four funnels.

I have already established that preparing MLPQs or dialogue-probing questions is a snap. But people generally run into difficulty with countering questions. Of all the skills you need to master, the ability to "counter" takes the longest to learn. It takes more time, not because it is difficult, but because it requires different skills from those we normally use. As a result, it requires a little more effort to master.

## How to Counter

As you saw in the scenario discussed earlier, countering questions are questions based on a prospect's response to a preceding question. The idea is to learn why a person responded the way he or she did. Counter questions ask people to explain their responses, to go into greater depth about *why* they answered the way they did, and ideally to get to the prospect's pain.

This has to be accomplished in a safe, comfortable environment. However, asking too many counter questions can create an interrogation type of atmosphere. My experience is that three or four counter questions ought to lead you from opportunity to change. You can use more, but ideally you shouldn't.

Counter questions can take two directions. They can either focus on the specific meaning of words used by prospects in their responses, or they can interpret what the client has said.

*Specific meanings.* Focusing on specific meanings is a lot easier than interpreting what a client says, but even this method requires some work to get it right. What you look for in the prospect's response are words that describe emotions and feelings. You isolate those words for use in your counter and ask the prospect to explain what he or she meant. On the surface, that seems easy. But consider what typically occurs when a prospect says something like: "Completing the project was very arduous. But, in the end, it was successful." The sales rep can then respond: "I'm glad everything worked out okay. What's your next step?"

Simple, right? Except that the sales rep here has missed an opportunity to learn more about the situation. Instead, he or she has asked the prospect, like most salespeople will, to focus on the future. But suppose the rep had countered with something like this: "You used the word *arduous*. What happened while you were completing the project that made it so difficult?"

Now the counter has several significant ramifications. First, it asks the prospect to go back to the past. This is atypical, and because it is, it will engender the kinds of reactions I've been talking about. The prospect won't and can't give you a recitation response. Also because the question is unique, he or she will look at you differently. And because his or her horizons are being expanded beyond the usual sales call conversation, the prospect will be more receptive to looking at his or her problems differently and will be more open to change.

I know that it seems like this one question is getting a great deal of credit, but of course what I'm talking about here is not just about one question. It's about a *process*, a process that began when you went out and did your research, when you established common ground with your prospect, when you got him or her to agree with your goal, and when you began the funnel. That's what began to set you apart from other salespeople and to make the prospect more susceptible to becoming your client.

The counter question is just one part of this lengthy process. But if handled correctly, it goes a long way toward moving you along to a sale. Again, what you are looking for are words that describe feelings and emotions, generally adjectives and adverbs, and when you hear those words, you ask the prospect to explain what he or she meant by using them.

*Interpretation counters.* These are extremely effective but require a finely tuned ear. Unlike *specific-meaning counters,* which flow naturally from what the prospect has said, *interpretation counters* require you to think about what was *not* said and to determine if there is a recurring theme and some personal issue involved.

For example, consider the statement that probably every salesperson has heard: "As a result of a very thorough evaluation, we've decided to stay with our current vendors and product line." Most salespeople will only hear in this statement, "status quo, case closed" and decide to move on. But what wasn't said in this statement may be very important, and that is why the company decided to institute a review in the first place.

Trying to find out what prompted the evaluation may not

lead you anywhere. Your case may genuinely be closed. But if you counter along this line, you've still got the prospect talking, thinking, and explaining. What you might come up with is some other avenues to approach the sale: "Was there a problem?"; "Is there political pressure?"; "Is there a new person in a position?" This kind of questioning is critical to getting closer to your client, understanding his or her difficulties, and coming up with a way to resolve them.

Another interpretation counter involves identifying a trend, a common thread in the prospect's statements. For example, if the prospect uses the expression *reducing costs* several times over the course of a short time period, it might be extremely productive to counter with something like: "You've used phrases such as *cost savings* and *reducing costs* several times in the last few minutes. It seems to me that this is probably a major thrust of your company now. Can you describe for me what precipitated this position?"

Finally, there are *feeling* issues that can be used to frame counter questions. These counters attempt to probe a prospect's convictions, attitudes, biases, and motivation. For example:

*Prospect:* The accounting department figures cutting the number of our vendors by one-third can reduce costs by 50 percent.
*Sales rep:* You say the accounting department initiated the change. What's your position on it?

Be careful here. You cannot assume that the prospect has a position, one way or the other. If you ask something such as, "Gee it's sounds like you're against the move," you risk backing your prospect into a corner. But offering him or her the option of saying, "Yes, I like the change" or "No, I don't agree with it" is perfectly all right and may reveal important information to you.

Finally, another counter covers what I call development issues, and it is intended to draw out a broader explanation of a narrow subject. For example, let's say a client tells you, "We have narrowed down our choices to either expanding our existing facility here or relocating our production to a plant we own in the south." A proper developmental-counter question is: "You say the two alternatives you're considering are expansion here or relocating production to the south. What were the other alternatives that you discarded, and what made you settle on one of these two choices?"

Asking a developmental counter question helps you understand the decision-making process that your prospect goes through. And knowing this process will help you sell more effectively.

## Some More Funneling Tips

Each time I've introduced a new technique, I've suggested that it is a lot easier than it looks. I am not doing that now. Countering is difficult. To a certain degree, it is intuitive, like the way a singer reaches for the proper note or a musician, having heard a song just once, can play it. Or, going back to my sports analogies in the Preface, some salespeople counter the way Ted Williams hits a curve ball or the way Billie Jean King returns a sharp backhand. For some, countering just comes naturally. They probably can't explain how they do it. They just see the ball bigger than the rest of us or hear the note more clearly.

But, obviously, just because you don't see the seams of a ball coming at you doesn't mean you can't play. Funneling and countering are very important skills. And even if you're just playing the recreation league version of funneling and countering, it's important that you at least are making the attempt and not just sitting in the stands and watching as others participate.

Not surprisingly, the more you play, the better you become. The most important skill you need to develop is your ability to listen. Very often when people ask questions, they're only half listening to a response. More often than not, they're worrying about the next question they're going to ask. This is especially true of salespeople who are frightened to death of a lull in conversation. But that is counterproductive when you are countering. You have to listen because your next question depends on the answer to your previous one. Let your mind go blank! Once you ask a question, concentrate on the answer.

Wipe your mind clear of all other thoughts. Don't prejudge. Don't assume. Don't add your own thoughts. Write notes to yourself about what the prospect said, and jot down key phrases.

## Another Funneling Scenario

Here's another example of how a funnel might work. It involves a company that is attempting to introduce a total quality management program and a sales rep for a company that produces computer programs that increase production line efficiency.

*Sales rep:* On the one hand, there seems to be a trend in business today, supported by Tom Peters among others, to run a tighter ship and to keep quality high, while cutting costs. On the other hand, recent articles in *The Wall Street Journal* suggest that the new methods are ineffective and that hard work is the only answer. Can you describe for me the direction you're taking and how that compares with your thoughts of the past several years?

*Prospect:* We're actively pursuing a Malcolm Baldrige Award, and, in the process, we've discovered that there are several areas in our operation, including manufacturing, that need to be reevaluated.

*Sales rep:* It sounds as though you've been thinking about this for some time. Was there a particular problem that set the evaluation process in motion?

*Prospect:* It wasn't anything dramatic like the loss of a large customer. It was just that the industry was changing, and if we didn't change with it, we'd be left behind.

*Sales rep:* Share with me what you have found.

*Prospect:* We've discovered a few things. First, there are some repetitive tasks that can easily and cost-effectively be automated. Second, there have to be tighter controls introduced to avoid the kinds of costly overruns that have plagued us over the last two years or so.

*Sales rep:* What would be the impact on your operation if you don't achieve these goals?

*Prospect:* I think we would clearly be at a serious competitive disadvantage. Our share of the market would probably decrease, perhaps substantially, and we wouldn't be able to accomplish a number of goals in our five year plan.

## Some Funneling Exercises

This was an actual sales call I was on with another sales rep, and while I've tightened it up a bit to make it more readable, the essence of the call remains the same. Here you can see how easily the sales rep moved the prospect to recognize the need for change. I believe this particular prospect had recognized his pain and had a keen desire to rid himself of it, even before we came. In fact, shortly after this call, the rep closed a very large contract with this prospect's company. But whether the prospect cooperates or not, your goal and methodology have to be the same. Here are some exercises to practice and hone your skills. I'll write out some funnels and ask you to counter at various points in the process.

*Prospect response to MLPQ:* We're trying to put a new operation in place in the next three months, even though we're short staffed.
   Write a counter: _____
_____
_____

*Prospect response to MLPQ:* Our procedures for selecting vendors haven't changed that much but the way we look at them has.
   Write a counter: _____
_____
_____

*Prospect response to MLPQ:* In the past, we purchased exclusively on the basis of price. But we found that the few pennies we saved on purchases, we lost on returns because of poor quality. Also, having multiple vendors became very expensive.
   Write a counter: _____
_____
_____

*Prospect response to MLPQ:* Our accounting people have told us that we are experiencing substantial increases in the cost of maintaining inventory, and they think we have to do something to resolve this problem.

Write a counter: _____

_____

_____

*Prospect response to MLPQ:* We're asking some of our distributors to help us by offering just-in-time delivery, and we're also looking at ways to cut costs at our warehouse by managing the inventory better.

Write a counter: _____

_____

_____

Please take a moment to complete the above exercises.

Here are some suggested answers to this exercise. As difficult as it is, counter questioning is still very doable, and to prove that point, I've given two counter possibilities to every prospect response. Yes, it is a lot easier sitting here writing responses instead of facing the pressure of sitting across the desk from a live prospect. But as I've said before, it is largely a matter of practice. As your skills improve through repetition, you will see how easily they transfer to the *real world*. I suspect as difficult as countering is, your responses are very close to mine.

*Prospect response to MLPQ:* We're trying to put a new operation in place in the next three months, even though we're short staffed.

*Possible counter:* You use the word *trying* here. What's happening? Is there something hampering your efforts?

*Possible counter:* Balancing a short staff while attempting to move forward can be a challenge. Can you describe for me how it's going?

*Prospect response to MLPQ:* Our procedures for selecting vendors haven't changed that much but the way we look at them has.

*Possible counter:* What's prompted the change in the way you look at vendors.

*Possible counter:* You say your selection procedures haven't changed that much. What has changed in the process?

*Prospect response to MLPQ:* In the past, we purchased exclusively on the basis of price. But we found that the few pennies we saved on purchases, we lost on returns because of poor quality. Also, having multiple vendors became very expensive.
*Possible counter:* Since price is no longer the most important criterion, can you share with me what the criteria are?
*Possible counter:* Reducing vendors seems to be a trend in the industry. Can you describe for me the process you're now going through to eliminate some?

*Prospect response to MLPQ:* Our accounting people have told us that we are experiencing substantial increases in the cost of maintaining inventory, and they think we have to do something to resolve this problem.
*Possible counter:* You mention the accounting department's involvement. Share with me your views of the situation.
*Possible counter:* What are some of the steps you've taken to resolve the situation?

*Prospect response to MLPQ:* We're asking some of our distributors to help us by offering just-in-time delivery, and we're also looking at ways to cut costs at our warehouse by managing the inventory better.
*Possible counter:* You are identifying only some distributors. What were your criteria for selection?
*Possible counter:* You mentioned you're looking at ways to cut costs. What prompted the search, and what were other considerations?

A simple way of developing your countering ability is to practice on your friends. For example, let's say you haven't seen an old buddy of yours for quite some time. You notice immediately once you meet your pal that he has lost a lot of weight. When you approach this person, the normal conversation goes something like this:

*You:* Wow, you look great—what happened?

*Friend:* Well, I thought it was about time I lost some weight, so I started to exercise and watch what I ate.

*You:* Hey, that's great. What kind of exercising do you do?

*Friend:* Well, I swim a lot and try to work out.

*You:* Hey, so do I. As a matter of fact, I try to get to the gym at least four times a week.

Do you see what is happening here? In your attempt to engage a person in conversation, you end up talking about yourself. You go to the last quarter too quickly. Instead, you should ask your buddy how he is doing with his exercise routine, how often he exercises, what type of diet he's on, why he chose that diet as opposed to the others you read about, and so on. And when your buddy leaves the party, he'll probably tell his wife what a great guy you are and that it was good talking to you.

Now that you've conquered counter questions, it's time to move on to the final quarter of our model—presenting solutions and gaining commitment.

# Chapter 10

## *The Final Quarter: Presenting Solutions*

Charles Revson of the Revlon Cosmetics Corporation once said, "In the factory, we manufacture cosmetics. In the store, we sell hope." The sales call is your store, and certainly, part of what you're selling at this point in your sales call is hope. To explain what I mean here, I frequently make an analogy to a visit to your physician.

You're touched, prodded, and hooked up to a variety of machines by technicians with cold hands and finally ushered into the doctor's office. If you're like me, you are a little nervous as you sit there as he or she studies the results of the tests.

The doctor looks at the report, looks at you, and just hums, "Hmmm." Then he or she says, "You know, you really ought to exercise a little."

"But, doc," you say, "I run four miles a day, four days a week, play tennis and full court basketball, and I take the stairs to my office, on the tenth floor, every morning and after lunch."

"You do?" Then he looks at the test results some more and says, "You have to be careful about what you eat."

"But, doc, I haven't eaten red meat in four years. I'm on a strict low fat diet and every week have three days where I eat only vegetables."

"You do?"

Based on the doctor's statements, you know something is wrong, and you're more than just a little nervous. You want that doctor to say, "Hey, don't worry about it. A lot of my patients have this. It's no problem. I've taken care of this a million times."

At this point in your sales call, your prospect is the patient, and you are the doctor with a miracle cure. The prospect knows something is wrong. Remember, you've just gone through several funnels—optimistically as many as four but certainly two or three—that have revealed your prospect's pain, pain that he or she may have been hiding from him or herself, the boss, and perhaps others. What your prospect wants right now is for you to say, "Don't worry. A lot of my customers have this. This is no problem. I've handled situations like this a million times."

## Moving Into the Fourth Quarter

In the half of the quarter-half-quarter model, you do not do any selling. Instead you spend your time learning about your prospect and his or her problems. You do that by funneling, and once you've finished, your job is to summarize what you've learned:

"As I understand it, Mr. Jones, you want distributors who offer just-in-time delivery, you're looking for a software program that will help you better manage inventory in your warehouse, and you want to consolidate the number of vendors you deal with."

Or: "As I understand it, Mr. Smith, you need some qualified programmers right now. You don't have the time to check a couple hundred résumés, and you need qualified temporary help while you install a new operation."

"Yes," a now dejected prospect says. "I don't know how I'm going to get it all done. But somehow I'll have to." The moment the prospect agrees that there's a need for change, you immediately enter the final quarter of the quarter-half-quarter model.

Reminder: Before you enter the final quarter, you must summarize what was said in the first half, check for accuracy, and get a commitment for change. Conducting these steps will set you up for the last quarter and confirm in the mind of the prospect that it is necessary to change.

The final quarter presentation takes place in three steps:

Step One: The Solution Statement
Step Two: Presentation
Step Three: Review and Confirm

## Solution Statement

Selling is a transference of feeling. Individuals are motivated to change when the risk is minimal, so a statement that indicates your ability to perform certain tasks gains the prospect's attention and confidence. The solution step that begins this process of change has two parts. It begins with a statement of confidence from you followed by a summary of the benefits of your product or service.

The statement of confidence is your enthusiastic belief that you can provide a solution. The benefit summary lists the benefits that will accrue in the prospect company if it signs with you. You want to start quickly and speak smoothly while the prospect recognizes how much he needs your solution. The solution statement will go something like this:

"Mr. Jones, I'm confident that our experience in inventory management and our computerized just-in-time delivery system will enable you to reach your goals in cost savings."

"Mr. Smith, I'm confident our database of 4,800 computer programmers and technicians will allow us to supply you with the permanent and temporary personnel you need at probably less money than you are currently spending."

This is like the overture to a musical offering a summary of the songs (or in this case, benefits) that are going to follow. Now you should go into greater detail.

## Presenting Your Company, Services, and Solution

Effective presentations are centered on the concept of benefit/ feature selling. It motivates prospects to buy and provides a clear explanation of how your services provide a solution to their needs.

*Benefits* are what is derived from the use of your product or service that will provide a solution to the prospect's needs. It is important that the benefits pertain directly to the problems uncovered in the half portion of the model. *Features* are characteristics of your product or service. For example, let us suppose you are selling a car. One benefit might be safety, and features that are characteristics of the benefit are an anti-lock braking system, dual air bags, and a crumple zone that withstands collisions of up to thirty-five miles an hour. Remember, a benefit is intangible. You can't touch high quality or safety. But you can feel where the air bag is, examine the brake system, and touch the crumple zone.

### Distinguishing Features and Benefits

The following exercise is intended to help you perceive the benefits and features of your product and service. Please pick out the features and benefits from the following services:

"Our copier parts and service contract includes regularly scheduled maintenance, thus avoiding emergency repair from inadequate or improper servicing. This means a lower cost to you."

*Feature:* _____

*Benefit:* _____

"The participating doctors on our list are all board certified and participate in an annual review process. Completing these activities ensures quality care and proper diagnoses."

*Feature:* _____

*Benefit:* _____

"Our money access machines make it convenient to withdraw money anywhere or any time, allowing you to get cash when you need it."

*Feature:* _____
*Benefit:* _____

"Our molding machine is operated by just one attendant, not two, as is the norm for machines this size. This means reduced labor costs."

*Feature:* _____
*Benefit:* _____

Please take a moment to complete the above exercise.

Here are the answers, which I believe are rather obvious in this case. The benefits are in boldface, the features in italics.

"*Our copier parts and service contract includes regularly scheduled maintenance,* thus avoiding emergency repair from inadequate or improper servicing. This means a **lower cost** to you."

"The participating doctors on our list are all *board certified* and *participate in an annual review process.* Completing these activities ensures **quality care** and proper diagnoses."

"Our *money access machines* make it **convenient** to withdraw money anywhere or any time, allowing you to get cash when you need it."

"Our molding machine is *operated by just one attendant,* not two, as is the norm for machines this size. This means **reduced labor costs.**"

### Principles for Effective Presentations

The reason I believe that the methodology I've presented here works well for just about every salesperson is that it is malleable. It complements your strengths as a salesperson and generally doesn't require you to make drastic modifications to the way most of you sell, particularly those of you who have already adopted the consultative selling approach.

Consider that when I talk about presenting your product or service, you'll use the same skills you have honed in the past. The only real difference is when you make your presentation—after you've gone through the quarter-half-quarter model, not before. Your presentation will of course:

- Offer clear and recognizable solutions
- Be well organized, well prepared, and concise
- Differentiate you from the competition
- Explain your benefits, features, and advantages
- Be specific and well documented
- Be enthusiastic and passionate
- Involve and influence the prospect
- Flow smoothly

### Explaining Benefits and Features

Even with the best presentation skills, it is important to remember that even though you know your product and service backwards and forward, your prospect doesn't. Simple things that may be clear to you are often unfathomable to your potential client but are often left unsaid because it seems simple and obvious to you. You have to be explicit, and I suggest the following format:

- State the benefit.
- State the selling features.
- Explain the features in detail to make them understandable.
- Show how and why this results in an advantage to the prospect. You should translate every feature into a benefit or advantage. For example, ". . . and this means you can save thousands of dollars or reduce your labor costs."

Remember, too, that:

- Every presentation should contain several benefits.
- Every benefit should be supported by at least three features.
- Features can support more than one benefit.

What are the kinds of benefits most customers prefer? I ask people in my course to imagine they are purchasing a refrigerator. I tell them to make a list of what they're looking for. The answers I get are not surprising: ice makers, ice water dispensers, movable shelves, side-by-side doors, and energy efficiency.

But when the class tries to add value to the various items desired in order to reduce the list to the three most important components, three core elements always come up: quality, value, and reliability. This identifies a purchasing pattern. That is what people look for. And if that is what they look for, that is what we should give them.

*High quality.* When selling a service, this benefit relates to the talents, expertise, and knowledge of those performing or designing the service being sold. When selling a product, this benefit relates to the manufacturing process, quality assurance, design, testing, etc.

*Value.* Benefits translate into dollars. They include:

- Greater efficiency
- Increased sales
- Production continuity
- Protection of contract
- Greater turnovers
- Lower maintenance costs
- Lower operating costs
- Space savings
- Lower labor costs
- Less downtime
- Lower initial cost
- Lower cost in use

*Reliability.* Covers your company's reputation and services. In your presentation, you'll use an expression such as *greater peace of mind.* It's important that you provide proof for your claims. Be creative. Appeal to all the senses; models, samples, and computer audiovisual presentations are all valuable. Show in particular:

- Testimonials
- Test data
- Results of surveys

Always start with quality, always end with reliability, and what goes in between your value-added elements is what comes out of the funnels.

### *Benefits/Features Form*

I've found that the most difficult part of this portion of the process for many salespeople is to put the many benefits and features their products or services offer into a manageable format. Remember, a benefit is what the customer purchases. It is the end result of what your product or service does for him or her. The feature, on the other hand, is an element of a design, construction, or service facility that enables your product or service to deliver that benefit. For example, a person purchases an automobile for a number of reasons, such as better transportation, pride of ownership, economy of operation, or safety. These are benefits. A four cylinder engine is a feature that allows fuel efficiency.

To make the most effective presentation, you have to understand and utilize the differences between benefits and features. To help you, I have designed a form that asks you to list the benefits and features your company offers. Keep in mind when you're filling out the form:

- The average product or service should have no less than three benefits and no more than five. Where possible, combine two similar benefits, such as greater efficiency and greater convenience, under one, stronger subject heading.
- Every benefit must have at least three features. For example, a benefit providing less cost in use might have features such as low maintenance costs, less downtime, lower labor costs, and a lower initial price.
- Try to keep the benefits in sequence. Start off with benefits that relate to quality, followed by value and reliability benefits.
- A single feature may be used two or three times to substantiate a benefit.

| Benefit | Feature | Feature | Feature | Feature |
|---------|---------|---------|---------|---------|
|         |         |         |         |         |
|         |         |         |         |         |
|         |         |         |         |         |
|         |         |         |         |         |

## Reviewing and Confirming

In the third step of the final quarter, you should:

- Review the key issues—the needs outlined in the first half—and how your benefits/features address those needs and offer a solution.
- Seek confirmation that the prospect buys into your solution and presentation.

It might go something like this: "Mr. Prospect, throughout our conversation, you've mentioned your concern about the impact on your company of the new tax bill. I know that our expertise in IRS account analysis that I've demonstrated will be able to put your mind at ease.

"Based on our discussion, are you confident that we have the expertise and resources to find any and all tax savings that exist? Is there anything I haven't made clear to you?"

### *Closing the Sale*

Attaining acceptance, agreement, and commitment to your call's primary objective is relatively easy once you've gotten confirmation from the prospect. So your next step is to go from commitment to action. For example:

"Since you agree that my company's specialty in tax services can assure that ABC Company doesn't pay any unwarranted taxes, I'd like to arrange a formal presentation to your company's management committee." Or ". . . submit a proposal." Or . . . "have you visit our facility." Or ". . . meet your president." Or ". . . sign a contract."

Here's a scenario of how a final quarter close might go, involving a sales rep for a distributor of industrial filters and pumps:

*Sales Rep:* I'm confident that our patented pump system will resolve your problem meeting the new EPA regulations. At the same time, the low-maintenance pumps will prove to be extremely cost efficient.

I think what we're most proud of is the quality of our pumps. Each is manufactured from a high-grade 285C steel. They are tested at ratings three times what they are listed for. [Sales rep shows a chart here.] And the pump uses a patented, seamless construction that won an award for its innovation from *Engineering* magazine. [Sales rep shows a copy of the award]. These features provide you with the quality you're looking for, don't you think?

*Prospect:* It certainly looks that way.

*Sales rep:* But a point I want to stress is that we're not just another pretty face. We provide value too. That seamless housing I told you about has undergone rigorous field testing for the last three years, and they've proven to go way beyond the EPA regulations on leakage. The figures are on that chart I gave you.

The housing is maintenance free, so it lowers your operating costs. It's also manufactured in a controlled environment, so no foreign elements can get into the inner housing. That reduces the possibility of a possible breakdown and thereby lowers your repair costs. Again, if you look at that chart, you'll see we've run a comparison of operating costs with the competition, and we came out 40 percent below them.

So, to wrap things up, I think our pumps will provide an effective solution to the problems we discussed earlier. They'll help you meet EPA requirements, they'll reduce your costs, and they're easy to operate.

*Prospect:* You've certainly made a convincing case.

*Sales Rep:* When we first started, I said if all goes well I'd like to come back with a firm proposal for you. Can we schedule a time when I can come back, meet with the members of your purchasing committee, and present a proposal I'm sure you'll find extremely attractive?

What could he do? The sales rep was so persuasive, the prospect had to say yes.

# Chapter 11

## *Some Real World Tips: Resolving Objections With Questions*

I started this book by saying that I am a salesman. I've been, and I still am out there. I know what goes on in the real world and that not every sales call goes the way it's planned. Despite your best efforts and no matter how much you practice, some prospects are going to say something like, "I heard about that article. I understand it's very interesting and thank you for bringing it to my attention. But I have to warn you that I'm very happy with my current supplier."

If it isn't that a prospect is overjoyed with a current supplier, then he or she will throw something like, "I don't have a lot of time" at you. Or: "I've had a bad experience with your company." Or: I've just had my budget cut." We've all faced situations like those. These kinds of heartbreaking comments can come at any time during the call. I know how easy it is for a statement like any one of these to throw you off your rhythm.

Objections are a natural part of the selling process, and you as salespeople not only have to anticipate them but prepare for them in the same way you prepare for the sales call. At times, objections even represent an opportunity to learn more about the prospect, and his or her concerns, and to educate him or her about your product or service. The majority of objections you receive can be resolved or overcome.

117

## Dealing With Objections

How do you handle objections? Here's a case of where what you *don't* do is as important as what you do do. First of all, you've got to acknowledge the objection. Unfortunately, there's no way to avoid that. But, at all costs, you have to avoid reverting to a traditional approach by attempting to sell at this point in the call. For example, consider the prospect who claims to be happy with existing suppliers. Naturally, you want to find out why:

*You:* What is it you like about your current suppliers?
*Prospect:* We've been with them for several years. They provide great service, good quality, and are reasonably priced.

By asking why, you put the prospect in the position of thinking about what's good about his or her existing suppliers. When a prospect makes a statement like that, your primary goal has to be to reclaim control of the call. It's not easy. Understandably, the temptation is to focus on your viewpoint and to rebut the prospect's comments. "But *we* provide good service. And *our* price is cheaper. And *our* quality is better." Nevertheless, that just isn't going to cut it.

What do you do then? Here are a few rules for handling objections:

- Understand the prospect's point of view.
- Be relaxed when responding.
- Encourage the prospect to talk.
- Establish an atmosphere of problem solving.
- Recognize that the prospect is objecting to your position or your product or your pricing—not to you as an individual. Be polite and speak clearly.
- Maintain a consultative, nonadversarial approach.

## The Four-Step Process for Handling Objections

It is relatively easy to deflect almost any objection and regain control of the call. The best way I've found to handle these kinds of situations involves a four-step process. These steps are: *Align, Question, Resolve,* and *Check/Proceed.*

*Align* is a two-part process. The first part is to do nothing. Pause for a second or two to consider not only what your prospect's actual words were but also what they mean. Pausing also serves several other purposes. When you receive an objection for the first time, you tend to think about it before you respond. Simulating this with every objection will help you avoid the quick "shoot from the hip" reply. Second, a strategic pause keeps your clients from thinking that your reply was prepackaged. It makes it seem as though you take their objections seriously and that you did not already anticipate their objection and have a response handy.

Part two is to align with what the prospect has said. By align, I mean you agree with the *gist* of the prospect's statement without agreeing with what he or she has *actually* said. For example, the prospect says, "I'm happy with my present supplier." What the prospect is saying here is that he or she is getting good service, good reliability, and maybe a good price. Don't argue with this statement. Agree with the essence of what he or she says by saying something like: "Good service, reliability, and value are essential." Another example is if a prospect says your company is too big. The alignment is: "Receiving the proper attention and response is important." Then promptly ask a *question* that will deflect the conversation back into an area you can control. For example, "What do you look for in a relationship? What are your expectations?"

If it's done properly, you temporarily eliminate the objection because when the prospect answers your question, he or she is focusing on something else. This gives you an opportunity to present *your* ideas.

Step three is to *resolve* the prospect's objection. Most objections fall into three basic categories: misconceptions, skepticism, and legitimate gripes. Misconceptions are common because many products and services are complex. They are generally very simple to clarify.

In skepticism, the prospect remains unconvinced that your product or service will perform in the way you claim it will or that your plan will solve a problem. He or she is being cautious, looking for more information, and it's up to you to allay any fears and prove that what you say will happen. This is easily accomplished by providing statistics, references to satisfied clients, or demonstrations.

Finally, the prospect may have a legitimate objection. He may have a valid point about some disadvantage in your product or service or a way in which it does not meet his or her needs. It's hard to believe, but that does happen on occasion. These objections can be about almost anything, from cost to terms to processing times to product capabilities. And the only way to handle these objections is to show how the many advantages you offer outweigh the disadvantages the prospect objects to.

Finally, once you believe you have resolved any objections, you should *check* that the prospect agrees—"Does that make sense to you?"—and then *proceed* to the next step. If the prospect doesn't agree that the objection has been resolved, you'll have to run through the process again.

Remember: Any objection stops the quarter-half-quarter model. *You cannot move forward* until the objection is resolved. Once it is resolved, you go back to where you left off.

As long as the two of you are still talking and you're in control of the conversation, you have a chance to clinch the sale. But I know you understand, too, that a client who keeps throwing objections—roadblocks—in your way will probably not sign a contract with you. Some people just don't want to be sold.

I wish I could tell you that when you use my system, you clinch a sale every time out. But I can't make that happen. No one can. In my questionnaire, I ask, "If a client starts a conversation with 'I can only give you ten minutes' or 'I'm happy with my present supplier,' how often do you actually get an order?" The answer was less than 5 percent of the time by people who had not been through my course. I'd like to think that using my four-step system to handle objections will increase your percentage of success. If I may quote the great "salesman" Kenny Rogers, who said the immortal words: "You've got to know when to fold 'em, know when to walk away, know when to run."

If, on the other hand, you want to hold 'em, how well you align and deflect can make a difference. So, how well do you align and deflect? Let's see.

## Aligning and Deflecting: Real-Life Samples

Again, to properly align with a prospect's objections, the most important thing you want to do is avoid agreeing with the objection statement itself. As noted before, if a prospect tells you that he or she is happy with a current supplier, you obviously don't want to agree that the supplier is doing a good job. However, you also don't want to disagree and put the prospect in the position of having to defend the supplier.

Your goal must be to find a way to agree with the core of the prospect's statement while not agreeing with the statement itself. On the surface, anyway, this appears to be difficult. But you will soon see exactly how easy it is.

Here's are a few sample run-throughs that will give you an idea of how this can work. These are real-life examples from when I have accompanied salespeople on calls or near real-life examples from my seminars, where participants have acted out scenarios they have experienced. In this example, the prospect is an MIS manager, but of course this can work just as easily in any industry.

*Prospect:* We're happy with our current supplier.

*Sales rep:* Getting the best quality, service, and reliability is important. What do you look for in these areas, and how does it compare to criteria you have used in the past?

*Prospect:* I don't believe we're unique. We need a vendor who can diagnose problems quickly and recommend a cost-effective solution and who doesn't require a lot of our time and resources to do so.

*Sales rep:* You say the abilities to quickly diagnose a problem and recommend cost-effective solutions are very important for you. I'm curious why that's more important than a regular maintenance program.

*Prospect:* Identifying problems and implementing systems solutions is a problem area for us. It's first taken us too much time to recognize problems, and then it took us too long to come up with systems solutions to resolve problems once we identified them.

*Sales rep:* One of the things we're noted for is our Star System. It's a program we've developed and that is exclusive to us. It allows us to look into an MIS system, see whether it's healthy or sick, and identify areas where the flow of information or operating systems can be improved.

What I'd like to do is find out more about what you're doing now and briefly explain more about our Star System. If it looks like there's some logical synergy there, I'd like to make an appointment to come back and run a study for you that will show you areas where there might be some improvement.

What the sales rep did there was agree with what was at the *heart* of what the prospect said which was that having a good supplier is important. Then the rep asked some questions that engaged the prospect in dialogue and got him to talk about what he was looking for. The rep also provided a way to resolve the prospect's problem and then, by asking for another appointment, checked whether the prospect bought into the resolution. This was all accomplished using techniques we've been using all along in this book.

Here's another sample of how aligning and deflecting might work. First, here is the traditional sales format in which the sales rep rushes into the final quarter:

*Prospect:* Your prices are too high.

*Sales rep:* Actually, I think you'll find that we're quite competitive. What kind of quantities are you looking for?

*Prospect:* We order several units a week, and we expect to receive next-day shipment from stock.

*Sales rep:* Our price is 50 percent of retail list, and we can probably go lower than that if we can offer you a contract that includes all your regional headquarters. We have over $1,000,000 in inventory on hand at all times, and we ship twice a day to meet just-in-time delivery requirements.

*Prospect:* That sounds great. Give me a quote for two units a week and get back to me.

What's happened here is obvious. The sales rep met the objection head-on and in doing so went right into the final quarter, trying to close a sale rather than build a relationship. Did he close the sale? It's possible, certainly, but it is more likely that he's just gotten the brush-off. He'll spend time coming up with a quote and proposal, and that will be the end of it. Now let's examine the same scenario, handled with the align and deflect method:

*Prospect:* Your prices are too high.

*Sales rep:* Saving money and getting the best value is an important goal. What are some of the ways you're trying to cut costs, and how does that compare to what you've done in the past?

*Prospect:* We're in the process of going through a cost-cutting mode which includes the implementation of a just-in-time delivery system. Our goal is to cut at least 20 percent from our bottom line.

*Sales rep:* It seems everyone I've spoken to lately is going through the same thing. What prompted you to take this direction?

*Prospect:* The marketplace has become more competitive. We want to maintain the quality of our product, and the only way to do that in this environment is to reduce our costs of operation. We think this is doable if we become cost conscious and get our vendors to assist us.

*Sales rep:* Trying to lower costs and maintain quality can be difficult. How is the process going compared to the way it was conceived?

*Prospect:* It's pretty new, so it's hard to tell. Most of our vendors are cooperating, and we've been able to reduce our vendor base which seems to have cut our acquisition costs.

*Sales rep:* I'm certain we can assist you in cutting your costs of operation and acquisition by more than your goal. We've done some work with a few companies in this industry, and, so far, we've been able to reduce their costs by 22 percent on average.

I just need to get a little more information from you, so I can submit a proposal for review by you and the selection committee. Does that sound okay to you, or would you like to add something to the agenda?

As you can see, the sales rep adopted countering and funneling techniques here to get the prospect to accept receiving a proposal. I suspect it will be awhile before you feel comfortable enough to counter and funnel an objection, eventually but you will.

## Aligning and Deflecting: The Exercise

Here are some common objections from prospects. Try aligning here with the objection. I'm confident you'll be surprised at how easy the process is.

- You're really not different from everyone else I've seen.

_____

_____

_____

- I'm looking for several vendors in this area. Submit a proposal, and I'll take a look at it. _____

_____

_____

- I'm not sure we actually need your service/product. _____

_____

_____

- Our budget has been cut. _____

_____

_____

- We're in a vendor reduction mode. _____

_____

_____

Please take a moment to complete the above exercise.

Now let's look at some possible alignments:

- You're really not different from everyone else I've seen.
  □ Selecting the right supplier from the many who come calling is always difficult, especially in the current environment.

- I'm looking for several vendors in this area. Submit a proposal, and I'll take a look at it.
  □ Making an informed decision is important. I'll gladly submit a proposal.

- I'm not sure we actually need your service/product.
☐ Selecting the proper resources to assist in your growth is important.


- Our budget has been cut.
☐ Allocating funds becomes even more important in today's environment.


- We're in a vendor reduction mode.
☐ Selecting a source of supply that best meets your needs and reduces your costs is essential.


See, it is easy. I know you'll find the next part simple because questions are just about all we've been doing for the last few chapters. Let's now add questions to your alignments.


- You're really not different from everyone else I've seen.
☐ Selecting the right supplier from the many who come calling is always difficult, especially in the current environment.

_____
_____
_____


- I'm looking for several vendors in this area. Submit a proposal, and I'll take a look at it.
☐ Making an informed decision is important. I'll gladly submit a proposal.

_____
_____
_____


- I'm not sure we actually need your service/product.
☐ Selecting the proper resources to assist in your growth is important.

_____
_____
_____

▪ Our budget has been cut.
☐ Allocating funds becomes even more important in today's environment.

_____

_____

_____


▪ We're in a vendor reduction mode.
☐ Selecting a source of supply that best meets your needs and reduces your costs is essential.

_____

_____

_____


Please take a moment to complete the above exercise.

Here are some possible answers.


▪ You're really not different from everyone else I've seen.
☐ Selecting the right supplier from the many who come calling is always difficult, especially in the current environment.
☑ Share with me your selection process and the effects today's competitive marketplace has had.


▪ I'm looking for several vendors in this area. Submit a proposal, and I'll take a look at it.
☐ Making an informed decision is important. I'll gladly submit a proposal.
☑ Describe for me the key elements you want to address in the proposal and what prompted you to look at changing what you're doing now.


▪ I'm not sure we actually need your service/product.
☐ Selecting the proper resources to assist in your growth is important.
☑ What are the main areas of your operation that you want to develop?

- Our budget has been cut.

☐ Allocating funds becomes even more important in today's environment.

☑ Share with me what impact these cuts will have and how they will affect the future.

- We're in a vendor reduction mode.

☐ Selecting a source of supply that best meets your needs and reduces your costs is essential.

☑ Can you explore for me the most important services a vendor company can provide for you in your current mode and how that differs from the way things were when you were able to use multiple suppliers?

As you can see, aligning and deflecting can be a simple process. Some of the alignment and deflection questions are almost interchangeable. So with just a minimum amount of preparation and practice, you can meet almost any objection that a prospect puts in your way.

The most important thing that you have to keep in mind is that your objective is to engage the prospect in conversation, to build a relationship with him/her, and to use questions to make the prospect aware of his/her pain and the need for change. But sometimes even that's not enough.

## When a Prospect Says "No"

There are probably few less worse experiences in a salesperson's life than going through a call and having the prospect say, "No, I don't feel this is the solution for me." I'm a believer in the "if he or she has already said no, what else can they do to me" school of selling. So when I'm certain I've come close, I always follow up with some questions: "Thanks for not wasting my time. Now that it's officially over, can you share with me why you said 'no?' Was there a problem with the presentation?" I generally follow with more questions like "What would you do now if you were me?" Or: "Will you share with me what I have to do in the future to do business with you?"

My experience has been that a large majority of prospects I've called on appreciate the sincerity of my questions and give me an honest response. At the very least, I'll learn something that will make my next presentation go better. But there's always the possibility that with the prospect talking and engaging in dialogue with me I may be able to salvage the situation and turn him or her around. Maybe he or she will tell me what I need to do to turn a "no" into a "yes!"

# Chapter 12

## *Completing the Sales Cycle*

Planco is a Philadelphia-based wholesaler of financial products, retirement investments specifically, such as annuities and mutual funds. The company sells products offered by large insurance companies to stockbrokers, bankers, and independent financial planners.

Daren Connelly, an assistant vice president at that company has an outside commission rep sales force as well as internal sales coordinators, who answer the company's toll-free numbers. According to Daren, the sales coordinators "are responsible for solving problems, answering product questions, providing sales ideas, and selling products. They take calls from people who've sold quite a number of products as well as from people who've never sold an annuity before."

Speaking of his thirty-one telephone reps, Connelly explains, "They needed to question better, and they definitely needed to be able to listen better, so they know what questions to ask. But one area where we've really seen a difference is that they are more aware of where they are in the sales cycle, so they're now better able to build a relationship."

The sales coordinators' computer screens were redesigned, Connelly adds, "so we know at any point in time where [callers] are in our sales cycle which definitely gives us a better idea where we are. By having that information so readily available, the targeted questions you can ask to open up the caller are unbelievable. It's helped us build better relationships with the brokers who've called us."

The quarter-half-quarter model is the key to your sales success but *only if you use it correctly*. Clearly, it would be silly for

129

you to spend half of your third, fourth, or fifth sales call building a relationship with the client. If you haven't established a good, positive rapport by then, the chances of making a sale are not at all good. In fact, if you're on your third call and still only getting first-cycle key occurrences and action steps, this is a signal that you're not making the progress you should be. It's a sign, too, that it might be wise to cut your losses and move on.

It's very important that you use your time effectively. One way to gauge that is to check the progress you make on each call, whether in fact you really move on to the next cycle or just make a second or third call that merely replicates the first. If the latter is true, then you ought to move on to a prospect that offers more hope of a sales opportunity.

As you can see from Figure 2-2, the amount of time spent in each portion of the quarter-half-quarter model changes as the goals of the sales call change and as your relationship with the prospect deepens. Ultimately, the quarter-half-quarter model becomes the quarter-quarter-half model.

## Getting in Your FACE

In a typical five-call sales cycle, the purpose of the second call is to continue to learn and diagnose the prospect's problem. In many respects, by the amount of time spent on each part of the call and the use of MLPQs and funneling, the second call, in many ways, is similar to the first. One major area of difference, though, is that in the second call, your goals have changed. While your first-call goals were to initiate a relationship and to get an agreement on the need for change, your second-call objectives might be to arrange a demonstration and to meet other decision makers.

You should find out about other buying influences as soon as possible, particularly when you're working with major accounts, which usually are complex-selling situations. There are several roles you have to identify; I call them the "FACE" — people—the Financiers, the Appliers, the Champions, and the Evaluators.

The *financiers* are the people who control the purse strings of the company, and they may be the most influential in the group. The financier is usually highly placed in the organization and has the power and wherewithal to find the money for your solution if he or she wants to, even if it isn't in the current budget.

The *appliers* are the people who will have direct contact with your product or service on a daily basis; they are the ones who will be using it on the firing line.

The *champion* is your mentor. He or she is usually, though not always, the person you've called on and can be found anywhere in the organizational table. Though, of course, the higher up the champion is, the better your chances are for a sale. Your champion is on your side because of the relationship that you have built with him or her. The champion is also on your side because you've been able to convince him or her that your solution will resolve a problem that's currently bringing the company pain. The champion wants you to win because if you cure the pain, it will position him or her more favorably.

It is important to note that the person who starts as your champion may not be your champion at the end of the cycle. You may meet someone with greater influence who wants to be your mentor and who is open to supporting and fighting for your ideas.

Finally, *evaluators* are technical people who decide on the competency of your product. If it's a computer, they'll probably be from the company's MIS department and will determine whether the computers you sell can be integrated with the company's existing mainframe. If your product is widgets, the evaluators will probably be from the manufacturing department, and they'll determine whether your product meets their quality standards. Evaluators can't select you, but they can eliminate you from the running.

Ideally, you start to meet FACE people as early as the second call in your cycle, though, for many of you, that may be impractical. But in a five-call cycle, you certainly should have leveraged your relationship with the champion to get some additional people at call three, which centers around a product demonstration.

From a timing point of view, the second call follows the first call's quarter-half-quarter model. The changes, however, are in your objectives and the MLPQ and funneling process which is more targeted. You've already asked the basic questions in the first call; now you want to dig deeper.

You also can begin to inject more of you into the countering process. For example, when a prospect says he or she is having difficulty finding accountants, the regular counter question might be, "Why do you think it's more difficult finding qualified accountants in today's marketplace?" But on a second or third call, you could say, "Do you think the new tax legislation being considered in Congress is one of the reasons good accountants are becoming scarce?" Countering in this manner shows you are aware of what's going on in and around the prospect's company.

## Call Three

The third call is where the quarter-half-quarter model begins to change. As you can see from Figure 2-2, understanding the prospect in this call takes on less emphasis while presenting a solution becomes more important. In fact, building a relationship and presenting the solution should now take about the same amount of time during your sales call.

If this is the point in your cycle where you meet additional members of the FACE team, you should start this call off by creating common ground. Reusing the material you utilized on your first sales call—the issue or article that initially caught the mentor's attention—is perfectly acceptable.

Your agenda is to bring the new people up to date. It can go something like: "I've spent a lot of time with Bill [the champion], asking questions, listening and, I hope, learning about your situation. What I'd like to do now is review some of the issues we talked about, get your feedback on these areas, and any others you believe we ought to include, and show you what my product can do."

Again, your objectives will vary, depending upon your industry and the number of calls in your sales cycle, but typically, in a five-call cycle, they might be something like: resolving last minute problems and assuming everything goes well and setting up another appointment at which you make a proposal. In the half segment, you'd:

- Summarize the information from prior calls that you mentioned in the agenda, state the information in a bulleted format, and ask if anything should be added.
- Get all the issues on the table and deal with opposition from anyone attending the meeting.
- Seek confirmation that a problem does exist and that a solution is necessary. This is a very important moment. *Getting all the players to agree that there's a need for change virtually assures that changes will occur.*

In the final quarter, you:

- Present your solution
- State the features of your product or service vis-à-vis its quality, value, performance, and cost savings while providing documentation and references that support your claim
- Arrange an agreement for another appointment at which you present your proposal

## Sales Call Four: Presenting the Proposal

The quarter-half-quarter model takes on a completely different mien for the last two calls in the cycle. I'm not a fisherman, but I imagine these final meetings are a lot like what a fisherman experiences standing on the banks of a stream, a trout just inches from his or her lure about to strike. It's exciting. It's what will make standing in the cold for hours on end worthwhile. But it also is a very dangerous time. One wrong move, and you'll frighten the fish.

By now, I hope, you can pretty much fill in the agenda for call four yourself. It's simple: Present and evaluate the proposal solution. You gain interest by telling prospects how excited you are with what you've worked out and how certain you are that the proposal solution they are about to hear will excite them too. Your objective, of course, is to schedule a final, follow-up meeting where they will purchase the product or service.

In the *half* part of the model, you should:

- Review all key issues.
- Review criteria.
- Describe any test results.
- Discover and deal with any last minute resistance.

The final quarter is your most important test:

- Thoroughly explain the proposal.
- Highlight the benefits of your product or service and how its application will lead directly to a solution to the company's problem.
- Sell the value, reliability, and quality of the product or service.
- Summarize the problem.
- Schedule a follow-up meeting to arrange terms.

You will also have to ask four more questions that are especially helpful in price-sensitive negotiations. These questions are intended to help you determine how you are positioned against the competition and what the prospect thinks of you. They should be asked in order and should be personalized to fit you, your product, and your prospect. They are:

1. Do you like what we offer?
2. Do you think we have the best product or service to meet your needs?
3. Are you comfortable with our understanding of your needs?
4. Do you feel we have the best resources to support you now and in the long term?

At this point in the cycle, all the prospect's answers to these questions should be positive. Positive answers obviously mean that you are a leading contender for a new contract or as a replacement for an existing supplier. A negative answer to any of these questions identifies an area of weakness that you have to focus on before ending the call. For instance, a negative answer to the first two questions indicates that your presentation needs some improvement in the fourth quarter and that you have not presented your product or service properly. A negative answer to the last two questions indicates that part of your relationship, the listening and learning part (the half), needs more work.

## Fifth Call

Life would be perfect if it were made up exclusively of fifth calls in a five-call cycle. In the opener to this call, you express your personal excitement at the prospect of closing the deal. Your agenda is to review the proposal and any other data pertaining to the contract and the relationship between the prospect's company and yours. You gain interest by assuring prospects that they have made a wise decision, and you might give some examples of past successes to encourage them.

In the half portion of the quarter-half-quarter model, you review details of the proposal and discover and respond to any last minute questions. In the final quarter:

- Review how your product or service will solve the problem.
- Determine application of your product or service.
- If necessary, seek confirmation of training seminars for workers.
- Finally, sign or release purchase order!

There are two important points that need to be made here. First, the steps I've shown you are only *guidelines*. We all have different sales cycles, different products, and different approaches. For some of you, meeting FACE people is unnecessary. One person may have full authority to order your product. For others, a demonstration may be impractical, but you may want to have the third call take place at your factory, so prospects can tour your production line and evaluate your quality control.

One of the reasons I was attracted to sales is that I consider it an outlet for my creativity. The salespeople I've met are among the most creative people I know. I'm confident that you all have the flexibility to adapt these guidelines to your situation. Just remember you should always state an objective that prompts you for your next step in the sales cycle.

Finally, second, just because you've signed a contract doesn't mean that the process is over. On the contrary, it's just begun, as we'll see in the next chapter.

# Chapter 13

## *Servicing Your Existing Client Base*

Mark Besca is a partner at Ernst & Young, one of the big six accounting firms. The company employs 64,000 people worldwide, has 600 offices around the globe, and annual revenues of $5.7 billion. It is no longer just an accounting firm, Besca says. "We call ourselves the world's leading integrated professional services firm."

Because of increased competition, Ernst & Young accountants do double duty as salespeople. Obviously, part of their responsibility is to land new accounts. But, as important, is that they uncover *existing problems and needs* at companies that already are clients to assist them with what Besca calls nontraditional businesses, such as actuarial or consulting services.

Besca, who concentrates on the company's media and entertainment group, applies the questioning and funneling process to uncover opportunities. He explains:

> A publisher may be having a problem because authors are complaining their royalty statements don't seem to be coming in accurately. If someone tells me that, I'd introduce him or her to the person we have who specializes in royalty systems.
>
> But of course that's not the way the problem is usually presented. It's more like, "Oh, here's that author again. He's a pain in the neck." Well, if you ask the right questions you'll find out why he's a pain in the neck: He's having a problem reconciling his roy-

alty statements. And if you ask additional counter questions, you may also uncover that this is perceived to be a problem by some or many of the publishing company's other authors. And if you ask more questions, you may respond to client challenges with the goal of adding value and making a sale. Also, you become involved in their business, and clients love that.

I can't tell you how important relationships and building trust is. Clients have called me and said, "We're having such and such a problem. Is there anyway you can help us?"

What Mark has done so very successfully is build a bridge of trust with many of his clients who turn to him whenever they have a problem to see if he, or Ernst & Young, has a solution. It goes back to what I mentioned back in Chapter 2: Your goal is to become your client's friend. And once you develop this business friendship, it's extremely important that, as Mark has done, you continue to nurture it.

Obviously, the first thing you have to recognize is that your number one, longtime client is your competition's number one, longtime prospect. At least this should be obvious, but too often, in the race to procure new business and in the rush to sign up every prospect in the entire world, we have a tendency to take existing clients for granted.

If you begin to slack off and find yourself no longer in control of your sales calls or able to engage the client in the same way that won you the business in the first place, you're leaving an opening for someone else to take your place. Like an athlete, you have to remain sharp, not only to maintain your existing level of business but also, as Mark Besca does, to discover new sales opportunities that a client may reveal to you.

However, you don't have to be sharp just because you want to protect your client from outside predators. Remember also that *your greatest opportunity for a sale is with an existing client!* If we as salespeople have a problem, it is that we don't sufficiently leverage existing relationships to cross sell other products and services our company offers. You are dealing with a client who presumably likes you, your company, and at least one of your products. Take advantage of this. Don't get sloppy.

Even if you know the client and his or her family intimately, and socialize with them outside the office, *the basic rules do not change!* Even though there will be some differences in the way you apply it, you still must follow the quarter-half-quarter model, you still have to ask multi-layered-probing questions, and you still have to funnel.

## Maintaining the Model

By now I hope you recognize that I am not a genius. Moreover, I expect that, at this point, you also understand that you don't have to be a rocket scientist to master this program. It is just common sense. So, here are some commonsense rules to remember:

- No matter how long, or how successfully, you've been calling on a client, the basic elements of the quarter-half-quarter model don't go away. I know I just said that a few paragraphs ago, but this is important! And it's worth repeating.

In a maturing relationship, there is a tendency to take the easy route. After all, we've already done all the discovery research in our earlier calls. We think we know everything the client needs. After all, we've unquestionably established ourselves as his or her partner.

You say you'll never take a client for granted? Don't bet on it. I'll admit that I sometimes take longtime clients too much for granted myself. I've found that as my relationship with a client deepens, I talk more and listen less. This is a mistake, and it's important that you don't fall into that trap. Selling to an existing client is easier than making the first sale. But do not confuse *easy* with a *sure thing*. There is no such thing as a sure thing.

- Selling is a *discipline*. A good salesperson is disciplined. For me, a perfect analogy here is with running. I get up at six o'clock every morning to jog. It's not easy, at least for me. I look for excuses to turn over and go back to sleep. "I can't run today," I tell myself, "It's the second Tuesday of the month."

Or, "Friday, the thirteenth? Why take a chance and run on Friday the thirteenth? Or Wednesdays in May? Who runs on Wednesdays in May?" You get the idea. However, because I know I have no self-control, because I know how easy it is to get out of the habit of running, I get up early almost every morning, even on bad hair days.

It's important that you get up early too. It's important that you maintain the integrity of the quarter-half-quarter model and that you maintain sales discipline because it is really easy to turn over and go back to sleep.

▪ Clearly, you don't approach an existing client in the same manner you approach a prospect you are meeting for the first time. But, by the same token, you don't approach a friend in the same way you approach an acquaintance. Your presentation undoubtedly will become more informal. Being informal is okay as long as you don't veer from the structure of the quarter-half-quarter model.

▪ As I showed you in the last chapter, the further along you go in your sales cycle, the more the quarter-half-quarter model shifts from questioning and listening to presentation. But after you clinch the sale, the model reverts back to the beginning of the cycle with its emphasis on listening and learning. Keep in mind that every time you introduce a new idea, product, or service to an existing client, the quarter-half-quarter process starts all over again, just as if it was the first time. Be cautious; just because you have a relationship with regard to your current product or service doesn't mean it will extend into other areas without doing your homework. Remember the competition is trying hard to get in. Practice the method that enabled you to get in and maintain that practice in order to keep everyone else out.

So don't take anything for granted. However, with your existing client, introduce yourself, as you did at the beginning of your initial sales cycle. And because you've already established a common ground, you may feel it is no longer necessary to extend the common ground by referring to articles and reports about your client's industry. In theory, at least if you want to, now's the time to talk about the large fish mounted behind the client's desk.

But remember, doing your homework is what separated you from the competition in the first place. So, as informal as your sales call may become, it's still important that you have multi-layered probing questions prepared and that you have an agenda with clear and measurable objectives to gauge your progress. Your agenda must reflect your continuing desire to listen and learn.

Every relationship has its rocky period. There are delivery schedules missed, wrong products shipped, and other commitments that go awry. Clients remember these mishaps. If you stand behind your partnership pledge and if you work through these misadventures, your relationship will almost assuredly stay intact.

But chances are your client will become a little more wary than before. Reality is never as good as a promise, under any circumstances. Therefore, I contend that the "gain/interest" section of the sales call opener is at least as important after you get the order as it was when you first met the prospect, if not more so.

Here is a perfect opportunity to amplify areas where your relationship has been a success by referring to case studies, references, and data that show how and where your solutions worked, especially if there were some miscues.

- You must be prepared for objections. Just because you've sold a client once or even a dozen times doesn't mean you have a safety net. There may be internal changes in the client company. One of your competitors may have made the client a better offer. Or your company may have made one or two mistakes too many.

Remember, the trend is toward reducing the number of vendors a company uses as well as the increased propensity for clients to rely on their vendors to help find ways to meet goals and cut costs. This is another important reason that you should stay within the confines of the quarter-half-quarter model.

So continue to do your homework. Create meaningful common ground. There always will be something new and interesting you can bring up to create a common ground. State your objective and get a commitment for it. Ideally, unless there has been a major blunder, you will have no problem with any reasonable objective you may have. After all, if you've successfully sold your prospect Product A, why shouldn't he or she be open to considering an order of Product B?

## Changes in the Half Portion of the Model

The changes between the way you handle a prospective client and an existing client become more apparent in the half portion of the model. When I first discussed the subject, I suggested, regarding prospects, that the preferred way to ask multi-layered-probing questions was to begin with the fact, follow that with an observation, and then ask a dialogue-probing question. I suggested a few chapters ago that it was perfectly all right to reverse the order of the fact and observation, just as a change of pace. You don't want to fall into a predictable pattern that suggests the entire sales call is preprogrammed.

When calling on existing clients, however, I take just the opposite approach. I begin with the observation and follow that with the fact and a dialogue-probing question. Beginning an MLPQ with an observation makes it more conversational which is more fitting since you and your client should by now have established a good relationship. And the observation provides a smooth transition into the fact.

Yet, it's a good idea to occasionally vary the structure of your MLPQs with existing clients. Again, the idea is that you don't want to appear preprogrammed. Sincerity is the stuff long-term relationships are based on.

While the structure of MLPQs may be changed, the content of these questions shouldn't:

- The fact must still come from a credible source.
- You must still continue to do your research.

I can't emphasize enough that research is what enables you to structure a good question. And by a good question, I mean a question that ultimately allows you to discover if the client has a problem in an area where you can provide a solution.

It's also important that you still follow the rules of funneling. Even with a mature relationship, I suggest that three or four funnels be pursued. If you want to increase your business, it is essential that the existing client recognizes the importance of change and the implications of not addressing new issues.

However, while the basic rules of funneling are the same with an existing client, there are still some subtle differences. One major difference is in the *intensity* of countering. Instead of countering on almost every issue, as you did when the client was a prospect, you should now be more selective.

Also, earlier on I said that three counter questions ought to get you to the bottom of the funnel, although it could take more. Nevertheless, with an existing client, the countering process should never take more than three questions. If it does, it will take on negative overtones.

There are a couple of reasons for this. First, given your experience with your customer, you should by now have a pretty good understanding of what motivates him or her to make a purchasing decision and what his or her "hot buttons" are. That's something you didn't know the first time around and that forced your countering to be more global and more all encompassing.

Second, even if you don't know all the answers, your customer expects you to be more knowledgeable than you were in the first sales cycle and certainly to know more how to get your client's first piece of business than another vendor would.

This creates a kind of interesting balancing act for you. You have to appear knowledgeable while still trying to get as much new and useful information out of the client as possible. Your counter questions, therefore, must be more targeted and more focused. Also you should apply the funneling process in a more exacting manner. In addition, your relationship with your client ideally should be such that you can more quickly move him or her from the top to the bottom of the funnel and to the final question, "What happens if everything remains the same?"

Because of this relationship, gaining a commitment is frequently just a formality, but you still have to get one, even when it seems superfluous. For example, if a client calls you and asks you for assistance in coming up with a solution for a problem, it may seem awkward, repetitive, and perhaps even counterproductive to ask if the client really wants to change. Of course, he or she wants to change. Isn't that why he or she called? Unfortunately, this isn't always so.

Customers sometimes take advantage of existing relationships. There are some who believe that giving you business entitles them to have you run around on special projects that are time-consuming for you but aren't necessarily at the top of their priority list. So, if you don't get a strong commitment, you may find your sales process delayed here.

## The Final Quarter: Closing Another Sale

If you've followed the quarter-half-quarter model, asked the right counter and MLPQ questions, and you've funneled, the final quarter is the easiest part of the process. It is important to remember, though, that the ease with which you get a client to sign on the dotted line is as much due to your track record as it is to your sales effort.

If you haven't provided the quality product or service you promised in your initial sales cycle and if you don't care the way you said you would, you could be the best salesperson in the world, and you still won't close another deal.

But this is a double-edged sword. Having delivered everything you promised you would, you're still not guaranteed another sale. You must continue to qualify the prospect, continue to seek action steps, look for key occurrences, and follow the models outlined here.

You have to keep reminding yourself to do these things. I know from personal experience. I was overconfident when I met with the new vice president of training at an existing client company. I'd been told how happy the client was with the work I'd done, and how the company wasn't looking at anyone else. And then I got confident.

When I met with the vice president, I didn't look for any

action steps and I didn't look for any key occurrences. When this client said he wanted an in-depth proposal, I told him it was no problem and spent close to a week getting it ready. That was, as I write this, over thirty phone calls, three dinner invitations, and two golf outing invitations ago—and more than a year has gone by. Nothing has happened. And I have no one to blame but myself.

# Chapter 14

## *Some Final Thoughts*

I was giving a seminar once, and one of the participants raised his hand to ask a question he was sure would stump me and probably get him a good laugh in the process. He asked:

"You mean, if I go into a prospect's office, and he tells me he's going to give me a big order, I have to turn him down? I have to say, 'Gee, I'm sorry I can't take your order until we get to know each other better. I need to ask you some questions first.' "

The participant did get a laugh, even from me. And of course I don't expect anyone to turn an order down. But to take the order, I told the class, and walk away is shortsighted. While you have one order, failure to engage the client and to continue building a rapport will hurt future efforts for more and, perhaps, even larger orders.

Let's suppose you received an unexpected requisition because a company's vendor was temporarily backlogged. Or suppose there was a fire that placed the primary supplier temporarily out of business. When that supplier resumes its service, you're the one who is going to be out of business. The only shot you have at making this temporary customer a regular client is to follow the quarter-half-quarter model, ask the questions, engage the client, and build a relationship.

So again no, you don't have to turn an order down, but, yes, you still have to engage the client. What I suggest is that you try to find out what prompted him or her to make the purchase, whether temporary supply interruptions are becoming the norm rather than the exception, and if this might not be an opportunity to alleviate the pain of going from one emergency to another by simply considering a new supplier.

Keep in mind that no matter the circumstances, you still have to stay within the framework of the models presented here. Certainly there is room for flexibility and for innovation, but the basic contours of the models remain the same.

Typically, when a company hires me to give a seminar, I plan my program specifically to that industry. For example, if a pharmaceutical company wants me to address its salespeople, I do not provide the same seminar as I do if I'm hired by a telecommunications company. That would be silly.

However, if you attended both seminars, you would see how strikingly similar they are because the basic steps are the same. In writing this book, though, I did not have the luxury of tailoring it to the way a salesperson in a specific industry sells. Therefore, it had to be general. So while it's perfectly all right to tailor the program to your own specific needs, you cannot lose sight of the basic outline.

Whether you're calling on a physician who only has a few minutes between patients, a building contractor whose office is the hood of a pickup truck, or an executive who has cleared his or her schedule for an hour to give you enough time to state your case, the rules of the quarter-half-quarter model and dialogue-probing questions should still be followed.

Whatever the sales scenario and whatever the product or service you sell, you must still engage your prospects in an in-depth dialogue, and you must still get them to recognize the need for change and to listen to the solution you offer to relieve their pain. You have to control the sale, and you have to pace yourself effectively. You cannot sell prematurely.

You also have to build a relationship, and make use of the funneling process. And at the very least, you have to try to use a multi-layered-probing question. No matter how little time you have with the prospect, asking one good MLPQ sets the stage for the quarter-half-quarter model and the consultative selling approach. Once the question engages the prospect, the focus of the sales call will be on the prospect, not on you. This is especially true if the question is a good one, one that literally forces the prospect to stop and think before he or she responds.

There are other advantages to using an MLPQ as well. One advantage is that you are controlling the call and setting the agenda. Another is that the prospect's responses give you an opportunity to funnel and to explore ideas and concepts that the prospects may not previously have considered.

## Some Real World Examples

There are a number of thoughts I want to leave you with, and among the most important is that this is not a "pie-in-the-sky" formula here. The quarter-half-quarter model, funneling, and multi-layered-probing questions all work out there in the real world. Here are a few examples.

In one of my courses, three salespeople worked for a food preparatory company—they sold soup base and similar items to restaurant chefs. During the course of the seminar, they told me they thought my concept was good but that it wouldn't work for them.

They made cold calls on chefs, they explained. But the cooks, busy preparing for the next meal, were usually not expecting them, and were very often satisfied with their current suppliers. Because of the time constraints and because the chefs were satisfied with their suppliers, these three salespeople felt they were constantly swimming upstream, and they didn't have the time to apply my techniques.

They felt they only had time to provide the chef with information about new products or improvements to the existing line—a new soup base, a base with better ingredients, or one that could be prepared more quickly. But there was no way they could state an opener, create common ground, ask a host of MLPQs, funnel, and present a solution.

I told them they were right; in their sales situation, there apparently wasn't sufficient time to do everything the model calls for. But that doesn't negate the fact that parts of the model could work for them, even with the limited amount of time available.

It was clear, though, that their current selling practices certainly weren't working. Blurting out their products' new feature immediately put them in the final quarter and put control of the call squarely with the chef. They didn't engage the chef and not having enough time is not a sufficient excuse.

Getting in an MLPQ may be enough, however, to start the process going. One of the participants, in another seminar, told me he would be unable to attend the middle of three sessions because of a prior appointment with a client. When he returned, he was very excited and couldn't wait to talk to me. Let me preface what he told me by explaining that he was both experienced and successful from doing his job for over twenty years and, I discovered later, already earning well into six figures a year.

He told me that he'd been calling on a prospect for years. The prospect would never give him more than five minutes and purchased very little from him. This was particularly frustrating to this salesperson because he successfully sold to other divisions of this prospect's company at the same industrial location. So, on the plane ride to the plant, more as a lark than anything, he wrote out two MLPQs.

I don't think it will surprise anyone when I say that the MLPQs did the trick and the prospect opened up. Just one MLPQ, then, can turn a five minute sales call into a ten minute sales call. That may be sufficient time to get the extra piece of information the competition doesn't have. That may also be sufficient time to engage the prospect in the kind of dialogue that builds relationships.

## Flexibility and the Game Plan

Remember, the quarter-half-quarter model isn't written in granite. Again, to use a sports analogy, a football coach may have 150 plays in his play book. When he plays Team A, he may select forty of them to use as part of his game plan because he thinks they'll work best against the opposing team. He doesn't put all the plays in the game plan though; that would just be too cumbersome.

But if the game plan doesn't work, a good coach is flexible enough to make changes and to deviate from his original plan.

The same is true in selling. This is your play book. There's the first quarter model play. There's the key occurrence play. And there's the multi-layered-probing question play. Some of them are basic plays that you'll run in every game. Others will vary depending upon the team you're playing. But no matter what team you're on, no matter what team you're playing, you have enough material here for a game plan.

If the prospect says you've only got five minutes, spend a quick minute on an opener, three minutes questioning, and the last minute presenting a solution. That's pretty tight, but what you'll find is that if you ask the right questions, the five minutes becomes eight minutes, or ten minutes, or longer. Also you will find that prospects will become more willing to explore solutions and listen to your presentations.

Remember that the incumbent supplier is getting more than five minutes, probably a lot more, because of his or her relationship with the client. And you won't make any headway until you stop focusing on the incumbent's advantage and begin focusing on listening and learning.

Even if you have only five minutes on a sales call, you can't waste that time by telling the prospect only about what's new with your product or service. That's what every salesperson who calls on that chef or on that physician is doing. By doing that, you fall into the traditional final quarter trap when you should be engaging the prospect in dialogue.

One thought I want you to walk away with after you close this book is that in a world increasingly becoming the same and in a world where there are few, if any, meaningful product or price differences, *you* are the difference.

So be different! Be flexible. You need to stay in order. You can't jump to the fourth quarter at the very beginning. But because every industry has its own peculiarities, its own cycle, and because each sales call is different, create your own game plan.

If you feel four funnels are too many, then only use three, or even two. If you feel that multi-layered-probing questions won't work in a specific situation, then use dialogue-probing questions. Your focus should be on questioning skills, funneling skills, and on integrating them into your existing sales plan.

If you're not using these skills and your competitor is, you will be at a serious disadvantage. Think about the first time you used a computer or some other piece of high-tech equipment. Chances are that you felt uncertain that you'd ever master so complex a machine. Well, chances are that now you're comfortable with it, whether it's a computer or a VCR.

Similarly, you may feel uncomfortable asking MLPQs at first and you may feel that the quarter-half-quarter model has little application in your industry. But I predict that once you use it, you'll find your comfort level increases.

\* \* \*

I read in a trade magazine that building relationships is becoming increasingly important in the sales process. I know that I've found that as my relationship with my prospect deepens, the likelihood of my getting a sale increases. What's your experience been lately, and how does that compare to the way you sold five years ago?

Get it?

# *Index*

traditional sales approach
(*continued*)
 factors pushing salesperson
  into, 18–19
Trump, Donald, in TV interview,
  79–80
trust
 building of, 5–6, 138
 dialogue and, 52

University of California at Los
  Angeles, communication
  factors study by, 11–12

value, 112–113
vendor-customer relationship
  building, xi
 *see also* relationship building
vocal elements, influence of, 11

Weidenauer, Bernie, on getting
  information, 70
win-win situation, 18
words
 influence of, 11, 12
 in sales approach, 18–19
 specific meanings of, 97–98